Cambridge Elements

Elements in Corporate Governance
edited by
Thomas Clarke
UTS Business School, University of Technology Sydney

INCORPORATING PURPOSE

The New Legal Foundations for the Corporation and Its Management

Blanche Segrestin
MINES Paris – PSL University
Kevin Levillain
MINES Paris – PSL University
Armand Hatchuel
MINES Paris – PSL University

CAMBRIDGE
UNIVERSITY PRESS

Shaftesbury Road, Cambridge CB2 8EA, United Kingdom

One Liberty Plaza, 20th Floor, New York, NY 10006, USA

477 Williamstown Road, Port Melbourne, VIC 3207, Australia

314–321, 3rd Floor, Plot 3, Splendor Forum, Jasola District Centre, New Delhi – 110025, India

103 Penang Road, #05–06/07, Visioncrest Commercial, Singapore 238467

Cambridge University Press is part of Cambridge University Press & Assessment, a department of the University of Cambridge.

We share the University's mission to contribute to society through the pursuit of education, learning and research at the highest international levels of excellence.

www.cambridge.org
Information on this title: www.cambridge.org/9781009623490

DOI: 10.1017/9781009623544

When citing this work, please include a reference to the DOI 10.1017/9781009623544

First published 2025

A catalogue record for this publication is available from the British Library.

ISBN 978-1-009-62349-0 Hardback
ISBN 978-1-009-62351-3 Paperback
ISSN 2515-7175 (online)
ISSN 2515-7167 (print)

Incorporating Purpose

The New Legal Foundations for the Corporation and Its Management

Elements in Corporate Governance

DOI: 10.1017/9781009623544
First published online: January 2025

Blanche Segrestin
MINES Paris – PSL University

Kevin Levillain
MINES Paris – PSL University

Armand Hatchuel
MINES Paris – PSL University

Author for correspondence: Blanche Segrestin,
blanche.segrestin@mines-paristech.fr

Abstract: In this Element, emerging legal forms of purpose-driven corporations are analyzed, revealing two important insights. First, within the traditional corporate law, a purpose is neither protected nor enforceable over time. While companies can have goals beyond profit, these are controlled by shareholders, who also appoint corporate managers. To protect social or environmental ambitions, especially during shareholder changes, a legal commitment from the company is essential. Second, these new legal forms highlight the need to redefine the corporation's legal foundations. In an era when management decisions impact entire populations and the planet, the law inadequately conceptualizes the conditions necessary for responsible management. The Element argues that embedding a purpose in the constitution of corporations can provide these new legal foundations. Ultimately, the Element suggests that purpose provides a unified theoretical framework for understanding the variety of corporate legal forms and for discussing their respective potentials and limitations in holding corporations accountable in the face of upcoming transitions.

Keywords: corporate purpose, responsible governance, benefit corporation, *société à mission*, corporate law

ISBNs: 9781009623490 (HB), 9781009623513 (PB), 9781009623544 (OC)
ISSNs: 2515-7175 (online), 2515-7167 (print)

Contents

1 Introduction. Corporate Purpose: Can We Rely on Corporate Leaders?

From all sides, there is a growing chorus of calls for corporate purpose today.[1] Scholars speak of a "corporate purpose phenomenon" (Besharov & Mitzinneck, 2023). Investors like BlackRock, nongovernmental organizations (NGOs), and strategy professors alike are championing this idea. Adopting a purpose is seen as a hallmark of social and environmental ambition for a company, as well as a strategic lever for mobilization, trust-building, and subsequent innovation (Gulati, 2022; Henderson, 2020, 2021). The calls for purpose are not merely instrumental; they also stem from the belief that the corporation is today the most influential institution of contemporary society and the best equipped to address the major contemporary challenges (Mayer, 2018). The economic capacity, but more importantly the research and innovation capacity of business companies now sometimes exceeds that of states: they appear indispensable in the face of challenges such as climate change, biodiversity destruction, and social inequalities.

In this Element, however, we argue that there can be no credible corporate purpose without a renewed legal framework for the corporation. This is indeed what is highlighted by the introduction of new legal frameworks for corporations in several jurisdictions, such as social purpose corporations (SPCs) and benefit corporations in the United States, and *le società benefit* in Italy and *sociétés à mission* in France. These companies incorporate a purpose in their constitution:[2] with this purpose, they will pursue both profit and social, environmental, human, scientific or cultural objectives. The emergence of such legal forms challenges the idea that the corporation is merely an economic actor. It also questions the idea that any company, under the traditional legal framework, is able to pursue purposes that are broader than profit. This Element presents the new legal frameworks of "purpose-driven corporations" that do not forsake profit but also commit on social and environmental goals and it defends two general theses.

1.1 Protecting Corporate Purpose

Firstly, we argue that for the purpose to effectively serve as a lever for transitions, it requires a legal commitment from the corporation. Companies that claim to have a corporate purpose generally do not include it in their constitution (or articles of association). Thus, the purpose is neither legally protected nor

[1] Throughout this Element, we define "purpose" as the goals pursued by a company, broader than profit. The purpose, as we use it, does not exclude profit but does not focus solely on it; it encompasses social objectives and ecological sustainability concerns.

[2] In this Element, we use the terms "articles of association" and "constitution" interchangeably (*statuts* in French).

enforceable and, in turn, it lacks credibility in the long term, even if it can genuinely serve as an instrument for strategic mobilization. This has been recognized for several years in research on social enterprises and "hybrid organizations" (Battilana & Dorado, 2010; Battilana et al., 2022; Ebrahim et al., 2014): these organizations face legal challenges because they must choose between a for-profit legal framework or a nonprofit association framework. However, usual theories of the corporation often overlook these difficulties and describe the corporate legal framework as open and capable of pursuing multiple objectives. Building upon different bodies of research, we will demonstrate that the corporation is, in reality, a legal framework that has become *asymmetrical* (Segrestin & Hatchuel, 2011). While it does not prevent the pursuit of social and environmental objectives other than profit, it provides no protection for such objectives, which can easily be challenged and put aside if shareholders change their minds – or change at all. Conversely, it allows companies to develop activities that have potentially a massive negative impact on society and the environment solely for the private benefit of their members, that is, their shareholders. Today, when companies like OpenAI have genuine collective interest ambitions when they set up, they need legal frameworks that are capable of protecting their long-term orientation for the benefit of humanity. The legal frameworks of businesses must be reinvented if we want to make purposes possible, sustainable, and enforceable.

1.2 Emerging Legal Foundations for Management in Business Companies

Secondly, newly emerging legal corporate forms are all the more important as they propose a way to establish new legal foundations for management within the business corporation. The legal framework of the modern enterprise, the corporation, was liberalized in the nineteenth century without, we will argue, conceptualizing the managerial function in corporate law. Historically, corporate law emerged before the advent of modern managerial functions. Many attempts have been made to consider management's responsibility to various stakeholders. However, in the classical corporate framework, corporate leaders – both directors and managers – have the duty to manage activities in the interest of the corporation. Legally, the interest of the corporation is open and cannot be confused with shareholders' interests. But since the corporation is an entity whose representatives are chosen by shareholders, the managers of the corporate activities will rationally pursue the satisfaction of the shareholders. If there are state-imposed rules to protect other parties and/or the environment, these are external to corporate law and to the constitution of the corporation. It can therefore be rational for managers to seek ways to circumvent them, as evidenced by tax avoidance. The challenge is therefore to establish responsible management *within* corporate law. The issue is not so much to contest the role and rights of shareholders but rather to build upon what is known from management science to clarify the conditions of responsible management. Modern management constitutes an extraordinary lever with which to conceive and implement unprecedented, profoundly innovative collective actions that have considerable transformative impact. It implies both competencies and responsibility. Purpose, we will argue, may be precisely the means to clarify these conditions and engage not only the shareholders but the company itself to adhere to them. A purpose, once incorporated into a company's constitution, establishes a foundational mandate given to corporate leaders that does not preclude diverse strategic goals: It sets out principles that corporate leaders must uphold in managing future activities. The purpose thus becomes a means of legitimating and regulating the managerial authority in corporate law. And if the governance structure is revised accordingly, with mechanisms to control management decision-making, the purpose becomes legally enforceable, both in relation to shareholder demands and with regard to other stakeholders. It allows for the respect of business freedom while defining limits or directions that will bind management in the company's future activities.

Building upon a growing body of research that links management, governance, and law (Battilana et al., 2012; Deakin, 2012; Grandori, 2022; Johnston et al., 2019; Leixnering et al., 2022; Mair & Rathert, 2021; Mayer, 2013; Meyer et al., 2022; Segrestin et al., 2019; Veldman & Willmott, 2019, 2022), we will argue that developing management that is suited to the twenty-first century's challenges necessitates new legal foundations of the corporate structure, which is made possible today by the incorporation of purpose, along with the new legal forms of corporations.

The new legal forms of purpose-driven companies thus merit particular interest, from both researchers and policymakers. They should be of interest to company leaders and entrepreneurs too. Statutory freedom actually allows for implementing most features of purpose-driven legal forms, but companies have long known that they can combine several forms together, or even invent new forms of governance (Mair & Wolf, 2021; Mair et al., 2020). The new corporate frameworks that are today introduced in law thus mainly constitute recognized legal models that may be shared, tested, and reproduced. The introduction of purposes into legal frameworks is a relatively recent option. It breaks with the multiple reform attempts during the twentieth century that aimed, above all, at a rebalancing of powers within the company among the different potential constituencies. The known alternative forms of companies are typically cooperative societies, where employees hold a majority share of the company's capital with democratic rules (one person = one vote), and codetermination companies on the German model, with a supervisory board where employees and shareholders can be equally represented. The explicit statement of a purpose in the corporate constitution is a legal innovation that appeared in the 2010s in the US (Hiller, 2013). However, prototypes can be found that were experimented with by local companies, such as companies with shareholder foundations. Today, however, there are multiple purpose-driven corporate forms in different jurisdictions. A unified framework of the different ways of organizing is necessary (Luyckx et al., 2022). We will propose an overview of the different legal paths to discuss their common points and their differences. Profit-with-purpose corporations have several common attributes (Levillain et al., 2019):

(1) they explicitly state a social or environmental purpose without renouncing profit;
(2) they enshrine this purpose in their constitution, giving it legal scope and extending the fiduciary duties of corporate leaders; and
(3) they adopt governance mechanisms to account for the respect and effectiveness of the purpose to their stakeholders.

But, beyond these common features, it is important to understand the differences between the legal options that are emerging. For example, unlike the French *société à mission*, benefit corporations do not change the governance of the company and require only that the company evaluates its activity against a third-party standard. It is important to discuss the respective potentials and limitations of the different purpose-driven corporations in relation to the socio-economic contexts considered. Ultimately, it seems to us that the design of governance structures will become a major issue, both at the legislative level and at the company level. We are thus entering an era where the boundary between management and law will blur and where disciplines will need to hybridize.

1.3 Structure of This Element

The Element is organized into four sections. Section 2 argues that purpose, if not "incorporated" or constitutionalized, is not reliable because not enforceable. It examines the legal conditions under which companies can pursue a purpose. It analyzes the theories of the corporation and how they have evolved during the twentieth century, and shows that they have not sought to challenge the law. However, these theories must now be challenged because classical corporate law does not effectively protect or enforce a company's purpose, hence the current interest in new legal forms of companies aimed at protecting a purpose.

Section 3 explains why "incorporating" purpose lays a new legal foundation for the corporation. It highlights the temporal gap between the liberalization of the corporation in the mid nineteenth century and the emergence of modern management at the end of the nineteenth century. The corporation was conceived with the idea of shareholders' delegates administering the company, not with the idea of modern, professional, and transformational management. We suggest that a re-foundation of the legal structure of the corporation has now become imperative to acknowledge this so-far-overlooked concept in corporate law: management. We then show that the purpose can be a means to recognize and bring together the conditions for responsible management in the constitution of companies.

But for the purpose to be credible, robust, and long-lasting, appropriate governance structures are necessary. Section 4 provides a critical overview of profit-with-purpose corporations internationally. It compares benefit corporations and the French *société à mission*, highlighting both their similarities and the profound differences in the nature of the purposes they can protect. Above all, it seeks to discuss the conditions for the effectiveness of these new legal frameworks, which must now be carefully analyzed, refined, and deployed to enable tomorrow's companies to effectively address contemporary challenges. Section 5 concludes with a critical examination of the conditions of corporate responsibility within society.

2 Why Corporate Purpose Needs Law: The Missing Legal Grounds of Corporate Purpose

In California, a debate took place between 2008 and 2010 regarding the protection of engaged and social or environmental entrepreneurial projects (Levillain, 2017). Specifically, "cleantech" entrepreneurs argued that their future shareholders could challenge the environmental focus of their projects. Even worse, they could denounce the environmental orientations as misappropriation or breach of fiduciary duties (Mac Cormac & Haney, 2012). Indeed, in most US states, corporate directors have fiduciary duties toward shareholders. These duties are subject to interpretation but generally include a "duty of care" (providing a reasonable amount of attention to business affairs), a "duty of loyalty" (maintaining fidelity to the corporation's interest), and a duty of "reasonable prudence" (Boatright, 1994). Some contend that directors who make decisions against the interests of shareholders are violating their fiduciary duties (Clark & Vranka, 2013). In the 1980s, as hostile takeovers increased, some legislators became concerned that directors faced litigation if they opposed takeovers that would lead to relocations and, consequently, job losses.

As a result, “constituency statutes” were adopted in several states that would permit or even require directors to consider various stakeholders in their decision-making (Orts, 1992). These provisions, however, have not been introduced in the two dominating states in terms of number of incorporations: Delaware and California.

The proposal to introduce a constituency statute in California in 2008 led to intense debates, prompting Governor Arnold Schwarzenegger to veto such a proposal, arguing that if directors could justify their decisions as benefiting any party, all decisions could be justified, leading to a risk of directors’ unaccountability. An alternative emerged: offering companies the choice to adopt a new corporate form that would allow directors to consider stakeholders beyond shareholders and specify social or environmental objectives. Two new legal frameworks were consecutively introduced in California, taking effect on January 1, 2012: the “flexible purpose corporation (FPC)” (see Box 1) and the “benefit corporation.” These forms allowed for a variety of purposes beyond profit, subject to conditions: any change in statutory purpose requires a “supermajority” of two-thirds shareholder approval, and for the FPC, directors must produce an annual report on their management of the corporate purpose for the general assembly (Levillain, 2012).

Box 1 The Californian Flexible Purpose Corporation (FPC)

The bill (Senate Bill 201) introduced by Senator DeSaulnier was adopted in October 2011. According to a commentator, it “encourages and expressly permits companies to be formed or converted from other forms to pursue one or more purposes in addition to creating economic value for shareholders” (Mac Cormac, 2011, p. 2).

The FPC differs from the traditional corporate form in several ways:

- The FPC has one or more social and/or environmental purpose(s) agreed upon between management and shareholders. The purpose must be written in the corporate constitution, which requires a two-thirds vote of each class of voting shares, with dissenter’s rights.
- The FPC must aim to “accentuate the positive effects or minimize the negative effects in the short or long term of the flexible purpose corporation’s activities on: i) charitable or public purpose that a nonprofit public benefit corporation is authorized to carry out. ii) The purpose of promoting positive short-term or long-term effects of, or iii) minimizing adverse short-term or long-term effects of, the

Box 1 (cont.)

corporation's activities upon any of its employees, suppliers, customers, and creditors; upon the community and society at large; or upon the environment" (California Corporation Code, s. 2602(b)(2)).

- Fiduciary duties are extended to include the special purpose(s). The FPC thus provides protection from liability for directors and management who make decisions on the basis of the agreed special purpose(s).
- The FPC is required to publish regular reports with objectives, goals, measurement, and reporting on the impact or "returns" of social/environmental actions.

It should be noted that the primary interest is not fiscal since, unlike nonprofit organizations, this type of company would be subject to the prevailing tax code (Corporation Tax Law, CTL).

Today the FPC has been renamed the SPC, for Social Purpose Corporation, and exists in California, Florida, and Washington State.

The FPC and the benefit corporation (formerly introduced in 2010 in Maryland and Vermont) are variations of what we suggest calling profit-with-purpose corporate forms (following Orrick et al., 2014). We will discuss the commonalities and differences between these corporate forms later. For now, it is sufficient to note that, according to lawyers and business entrepreneurs themselves, companies seeking to pursue a social or environmental purpose require a specific legal framework, thus prompting a reexamination of prevailing corporate theories.

As this section will rapidly show, several theories have argued that the corporation could serve interests beyond those of shareholders. Paradoxically, however, these theories, by postulating that existing legal frameworks already enable this variety of purposes, have long undermined the debate on changing the legal framework. According to their view, corporate social responsibility (CSR) corresponds to the actions of the company beyond its legal obligations, but within the existing legal framework. These premises are already being questioned by changes in the law, and it is these premises that we need to question theoretically today.

In this section, we begin by briefly presenting the debates on the "purpose of the corporation." Then, we review the legal motivations that led to the introduction of benefit corporations or FPCs in the US. This highlights the legal conditions for CSR that had not been met so far in the context of the corporation. And in a third step, we show how including a purpose in the corporation's constitution can support the fulfillment of these conditions.

2.1 The Purpose of the Corporation[3]: A Brief History of the Debate

Here we present a succinct overview of the debates surrounding the purpose of the corporation during the twentieth century (Gartenberg, 2022). The purpose of the corporation also pertains to the function of directors: whom should they serve and for whom are they the trustees?

In the 1920s, the power of large corporations had grown so significantly that concerns arose over the influence of directors, but also around the control of shareholders who could steer management decisions toward their private benefit while enjoying limited liability. Legal scholar Berle was among those contemplating how to legally frame those in a position of "control," hence the shareholders (Berle Jr., 1931). In a famous controversy, Dodd opposed this view, arguing that management was becoming more professional and that this professionalization meant distancing from shareholders (Dodd, 1932). He believed that it was more about recognizing directors' responsibilities, not only toward shareholders but also toward all stakeholders, without altering the law.

During the 1960s and 1970s, governance debates reemerged, particularly when corporate executives were accused of favoring their interests and building industrial empires to the detriment of company performance. In an era of sharp liberalism, economist Milton Friedman famously retorted that directors' responsibilities were only to those who hired them – the shareholders – to manage their affairs: "That responsibility is to conduct the business in accordance with their desires, which generally will be to make as much money as possible while conforming to the basic rules of society, both those embodied in law and those embodied in ethical custom" (Friedman, 1970, n.p.). This perspective solidified the doctrine of maximizing shareholder value as the primary goal of directors.

Clearly, the law states nothing of the sort (Blair & Stout, 1999; Lan & Heracleous, 2010; Mahoney, 2023; Robé, 1999). Instead, the economic theory of agency offers but one interpretation of the law: directors are in an agency relationship with shareholders (Fama & Jensen, 1983b), tasked with acting in their name and on their behalf. However, they might seek to act in their self-interest, leading to the necessity of monitoring directors and providing incentives to ensure that they work solely in the interests of their principals (Fama & Jensen, 1983a; Jensen & Meckling, 1976). Although legally disputable, this interpretation has significantly influenced governance circles and led to the drafting of governance codes. The first,

[3] Note: By 'corporation,' we refer here to the classic form of the joint-stock company as it has developed, particularly in the United States. This is the 'archetype' of market organizations for much of the 20th century (Meyer et al., 2022; Mair & Rathert, 2021). It has become the reference point in governance theories, even though other forms—such as codetermination in Germany—have also developed.

the Cadbury Report published in London in 1992, clearly reiterated the idea that directors must act in the name and on behalf of their shareholders (Cadbury, 1992).

In light of this, it is understandable that proponents of a more social and responsible approach to executive roles had to curtail their ambitions (Marens, 2008). The CSR movement gained momentum in the 1970s but stopped short of legal reform, despite strong calls to action like that of Selznick in 1969 (Segrestin et al., 2022; Selznick, 1969). Thus, CSR developed "beyond the law," imposing no legal obligations but emphasizing that sound management – within the stakeholder management perspective – implied considering the interests of various parties. Major scandals, such as the Amoco Cadiz environmental disaster in 1974, resonated with these considerations. Simplifying the story from today's viewpoint, CSR initiatives grew significantly, but mainly from an instrumental perspective, aiming at managing social and environmental risks (Lohmeyer & Jackson, 2024): directors were urged to identify the most "salient" stakeholders, those who could most impact the company's future (Mitchell et al., 1997). Properly managing a company meant effectively managing risks associated with stakeholders while maintaining a strong shareholder orientation.

By the late 1990s, the debate resumed. The excesses of shareholder governance became clear (Aglietta & Rebérioux, 2005; Gelter, 2009). The transformation of the shareholder world, marked by the arrival of professional institutional investment funds with entirely new management logics, played a part (Belinga & Guez, 2018; Klettner, 2021). It appeared in some cases that directors ensured high profitability by shifting business risks onto others (Clarke, 2020). For example, dismantling a group by selling it off in parts could secure exceptional dividends or massive share buybacks as detailed by W. Lazonick, or simply forgoing all investments with distant and uncertain returns (Lazonick, 2014). Ultimately, the shareholder policy turned against the company itself. Whereas shareholders were supposed to assume economic risk, they ended up in a position of receiving guaranteed dividends. And where directors were supposed to manage the company's development, they found themselves jeopardizing it. The "financial" crisis of 2007–08 was in reality not a crisis of financial markets but rather a crisis of corporate management, due to a marked shift in corporate governance doctrines (Favereau, 2014; Segrestin & Hatchuel, 2012).

In 1999, agency theory and the doctrine of shareholder governance were challenged on a legal basis: M. Blair and L. Stout, two eminent professors in law and economics, familiar with the economic analysis of the firm, disputed the corporate law interpretation made by agency theorists. According to them, a corporation is a legal entity with its own legal personality, the sole owner of its assets and outcomes (Blair & Stout, 1999; see also Robé, 1999, 2011). Shareholders own only their shares and cannot legally interfere with management decisions, risking the loss of their liability limitation. The authors argued that, legally, directors have a fiduciary duty to the corporation, not to the shareholders. This spurred a new trend of research that sees promise in the personification of the company. The goal, therefore, would be to restore the spirit of corporate law to define the role of directors, this time as trustees of the company, not just its stakeholders.

These cycles of debate thoroughly examined the "purpose of the corporation" and the corollary expectations regarding the board of directors. As T. Clarke (2020) pointed out, this "contest on corporate purpose" shows, with a few decades' hindsight, how the Friedmanian constricted interpretation has led both to social and ecological crises but also to jeopardizing corporations themselves. Nevertheless, in the end, while the legal framework can be interpreted differently, the role of the legal construction of the corporation should not be underestimated (Veldman & Willmott, 2022). The conception of the corporation as a third-party entity has challenged Friedman's restrictive interpretation of the law. But it has not called for changing the law, even in the face of renewed social and environmental crises.

2.2 How Current Law Impedes Corporate Purpose

In practice, however, as demonstrated by the introduction of the FPC in California in 2011, corporate law does not provide the conditions necessary for directors to pursue the interests of stakeholders other than shareholders. In other words, the law does not protect ambitious CSR initiatives (Levillain et al., 2019). Several arguments clarify this point, which are in fact the motivations behind the creation of the FPC in the US (Mac Cormac & Haney, 2012), similar to the *société à mission* in France (Notat & Senard, 2018).

Firstly, as highlighted, fiduciary duties can be subject to restrictive interpretations. Thus, directors, rightly or wrongly, fear legal action, and this fear often dissuades them from pursuing social and environmental objectives. One of the lawyers who originated the concept of benefit corporations, William Clark, emphasizes this in the white paper on benefit corporations. For-profit companies pursuing a social mission face increasing difficulty as they scale:

> [A]s officers and directors of these entities consider investments, mergers or liquidity events, the default position tends to favor the traditional fiduciary responsibility to maximize returns to shareholders over the company's social mission. Many leaders of early and growth-stage mission-driven businesses fear being pressured to change business practices or pursue strategic alternatives to independent growth by investors whose financial interests often diverge over time from the social mission of the company. Whatever the letter of the law, these fears, combined with both prevailing business culture and advice of counsel about the risk of litigation if one fails to maximize shareholder value, have a chilling effect on corporate behavior as it relates to pursuit of a social mission. (Clark & Vranka, 2013, p. 6)

A second argument is perhaps stronger: the future shareholders of a company are unknown. Social and environmental initiatives and investments are lawful, as shown by the Freshfield Report commissioned by the United Nations in 2005. However, such initiatives or investments require the consent of the shareholders (Sandberg, 2011). In a corporation, shares are freely transferable, making it impossible for the company to control who will be its future shareholders and whether they will continue to support social or environmental ambitions. Shareholders actually have various means to cancel these initiatives, for example dismissing directors, suing them for breach of fiduciary duties, cutting their pay, voting on resolutions, or engaging in public campaigns. In other words, current law does not commit shareholders to a corporate project and cannot protect a specific project without shareholder agreement. Consequently, we can suggest that corporate law is asymmetrical (Segrestin & Hatchuel, 2011): while it does not preclude social and environmental actions, it does not protect them. These can be challenged by shareholders, particularly when there is a change in ownership. It could be argued that the exclusive control granted to shareholders over directors legally blocks the potential for CSR. "In fact, to the extent management nomination and pay is arbitrarily and unconstraintly decided by shareholders, it is unlikely that management can act in the best interest of the corporation as a whole" (Grandori, 2022, p. 67).

A third argument must be considered: allowing social or environmental purposes would require expanding the scope of directors' actions and their autonomy from shareholders. But how, then, to ensure the control of directors? This is the dilemma faced by stakeholder theory. "An organization that is answerable to everyone, is actually answerable to no one" (Sternberg, 2000, p. 7). The proposition of a constituency statute in California was rejected on this basis: allowing directors to consider all parties would make them unaccountable, and thus potentially irresponsible.

This argument is significant because it illustrates the challenge of conceptualizing an alternative legal framework if corporations are to remain sustainable. The discussions preceding the introduction of the FPC in California show this: it was considered to have directors' actions controlled not by any one party – which could always realign the corporation's purpose with its own interests – but against an external standard of evaluation. This approach, as we will develop in Section 4, was chosen by benefit corporations. However, proponents of the FPC argued that a standard would prevent companies from pursuing social and environmental goals specific to them. Instead, they advocated that a company should be able to define its own purpose and commit future shareholders to this purpose by including it in the very contract of the corporation, that is, in its constitution (Levillain et al., 2019).

2.3 Constitutionalizing Purpose to Achieve Both Entrepreneurial Freedom and Accountability

Once we acknowledge that corporate law is asymmetrical – that is, it does not prevent a company from pursuing varied purposes but fails to protect them – the discourse surrounding purpose without any change in the corporate legal framework appears suspicious. A specific purpose, within the traditional legal framework of a company, is neither secured nor enforceable. Instead of inspiring trust, many stakeholders conversely deem it dubious. And mistrust is indeed legitimate.

This context highlights why new corporate forms emerge that incorporate both a purpose and a profit motive in their constitution. Constitutionalizing the purpose – that is, explicitly stating and including its formulation in the company's constitution – addresses the issues previously mentioned (Segrestin & Levillain, 2023):

(1) *Constitutionalizing clarifies and protects the purpose of the corporation*. The century-old debate about whom should the company be run for is then cleared. The previous notion that a company could have its "own" interest, as a distinct legal person from its members, did not permit a clear definition of this interest. If the only spokespersons for the company are directors who are elected by shareholders in an annual general meeting (AGM), then the company's interest is likely to align with that of this electorate. Formulating the purpose is therefore a way of specifying some foundational social or environmental objectives of the legal entity, alongside the expectations of present or future shareholders. It also serves to anchor this purpose beyond potential changes in shareholders. To change or abandon the purpose, shareholders must indeed pass a new supermajority decision in the general assembly to change the articles of incorporation, and as these articles are publicly available, it also makes the decision public, which will inform all stakeholders.

(2) *The purpose also clarifies directors' mandate and accountability*. The purpose established a foundational framework that sets the objectives that directors must endeavor to pursue and against which their strategy will be evaluated. In principle, unless contrary clauses have been decided, shareholders can communicate certain demands to directors, and they retain the right to revoke them. Nonetheless, an explicit mandate to pursue social or environmental objectives precludes potential lawsuits against a director who makes decisions in line with the purpose rather than in the shareholders' interest. The breach of fiduciary duties could no longer be invoked. Hence, the purpose provides directors with a "safe harbor" (Mac Cormac & Haney, 2012). However, directors are not unaccountable; they must indeed account for their strategy concerning the purpose. The difficulty that stakeholder theorists have faced to date is thus resolved, as

managers are no longer required to consider all stakeholders but must justify their strategy in light of the purpose.

(3) Finally, by allowing each company to define its own purpose, *the social and environmental commitments of companies are facilitated and rendered enforceable* while respecting corporate freedom. This is crucial because what is desirable or of collective interest is variously appreciated as long as there is no proper legal rule to prescribe certain behaviors. The law – or the state – can prohibit what is harmful. However, it cannot compel companies to create what is desirable. In the past, companies have shown that they could initiate projects of collective interest that could not have been decreed or decided by public authorities. Consider objects like the train, the telephone, or COVID-19 vaccines ... In each case, a private initiative was the origin of what is now recognized as of public interest. And it is a safe bet that the products or services that will be most useful to us in 2050 are still unknown and unimaginable.

We will enter into more detail in Section 4 to differentiate among the various options that legislations have currently introduced to constitutionalize corporate purpose, and to discuss their respective advantages and drawbacks. It is, however, important to emphasize here that a wide range of implementations is possible that can give law more or less "teeth" with which to frame the purpose's formulation, and to make it enforceable.

2.4 Section Conclusion: Key Elements

A corporation, as a legal person, can indeed have a purpose distinct from that of its members. However, until it is explicitly and legally stated, it is in practice largely influenced by the expectations of those in control, i.e. those who appoint and dismiss managers, namely, the shareholders. This is what we call a control dilemma: in reality, the corporation's purpose can be subsumed under the interest of those who ultimately control it.

Corporate law, having remained stable since the early twentieth century, does not prevent a company from pursuing a social or environmental purpose alongside its profit objective. However, it does not provide structures to protect this purpose. Corporate law is thus asymmetrical. A corporate social or environmental purpose without specific legal existence is therefore unprotected and lacks credibility.

If a company incorporates a purpose into its constitution, then it achieves multiple outcomes:

(1) It clarifies the purpose of the corporation and addresses the control dilemma, limiting the risk that the purpose is considered by management only contingently, and based on the expectations of the parties holding control rights.
(2) It addresses the asymmetry of the law by protecting the purpose and making it enforceable, even in the face of changes in shareholding.

(3) It enables the protection of directors from prosecution while preserving their accountability.
(4) It maintains, or even preserves, the freedom of enterprise by allowing for varied purposes and permitting the alignment of the company's purpose with the collective interest.

3 Revisiting the Legal Foundations of Management in the Corporation

The emergence of new legal corporate structures shows that many stakeholders, including lawyers, policymakers, and entrepreneurs, have considered that corporate law was not suited to promoting responsible businesses capable of addressing contemporary social and environmental challenges.

In this section, we analyze why corporate law is inappropriate and how the introduction of purpose, along with appropriate governance mechanisms, can restore the possibility of responsible business. We argue here that corporate law is unsuitable because it does not conceptualize the managerial function. In particular, it does not consider the conditions, in terms of competence, discretion, and responsibility, under which management can and should exercise its functions.

To understand this, it is important to realize that corporate law was liberalized and spread historically before the emergence of modern management. We must therefore return to the two movements that led to the birth of the modern business corporation.

And before that, a clarification is needed on what we mean by the modern corporation. The business corporation is often seen as an economic organization that produces goods or services with the aim of selling them and thus making a profit. This definition, while not incorrect, applies equally to a cobbler and a pharmaceutical company like Pfizer. It is also ahistorical, as it applies to both a baker selling his bread in ancient Rome and a Silicon Valley entrepreneur in artificial intelligence today! This definition is therefore far too crude to address the business corporation in the twenty-first century. The modern corporation, as we know it, with shareholders, managers, and employees, appeared historically quite late, roughly at the beginning of the twentieth century. Labor law, particularly in Europe where it is more developed, was codified only in the early twentieth century, for example. Thus, two movements were necessary for the modern company to emerge: first, the birth of the legal framework of the corporation and second, the rise of modern management. We will review these movements one by one.

First, we will consider the birth of the legal framework of the corporation, which notably allows for massive capital raising. In corporate law, those who run the business are the directors, who may delegate part of the management to executives. Fundamentally, they must run the business in the name and on behalf of the legal entity, which is represented by the shareholders.

Second, we will build upon research in business history but also in management sciences to underline that the modern company also required the emergence of a very distinctive figure, the executive or professional manager, with highly specific competencies, both to design value-creating strategies and to conduct collective action responsibly. The authority of management, to be legitimate, was recognized in labor law with new responsibilities. However, this did not, in turn, affect the constitutional order of the corporation.

Third, we will emphasize how these two movements result in an extreme ambivalence of the current status of managers – particularly chief executive officers (CEOs). In corporate law, directors are appointed and supervised by the shareholders. Chief executive officers are nominated by the board. Their managerial rationality is therefore normally oriented toward satisfying the latter. But at the same time, they are granted authority to lead activities and to direct others stakeholders based on the expectation that they will act diligently, and responsibly.

Finally, we will argue that the introduction of new legal forms of companies, such as purpose-with-profit corporations, points to a path for establishing new legal foundations of the corporation by clarifying the role and responsibilities of management in corporate law.

3.1 The Rise of the Modern Corporation: Limited Liability for All

3.1.1 From Partnership to Limited Liability for All

The history of corporations is complex and varied depending on the region. It is not our objective to present a detailed account. However, schematically, the modern corporation results from the combination of two genealogical threads.

The first is that of the partnership-based commercial company (*societas*). In the Middle Ages, it allowed several individuals to associate in solidum to form a single entity vis-à-vis third parties. The partners were jointly and indefinitely liable, involving their personal assets, for the debts of the company. Moreover, they could not transfer their shares: the company ceased to exist upon the death of any one of them.

Several developments accompanied commercial growth throughout history (Guinnane et al., 2008; Hatchuel & Segrestin, 2007; Szramkiewicz, 1989). First, shares became transferable to allow the company to survive its members and perpetuate the business. Then, the possibility for members to have only limited liability was authorized. The limited partnership (*commenda*) typically allowed associating capital contributors (limited partners), who risked losing only the amount of their contribution, with other members – the general partners – who retained responsibility for management acts. It should be noted that limited partners were prohibited from interfering in management decisions: any interference would make them de facto managers and revoke their limited liability.

The second thread is that of legal personality. In Rome, legal personality (*corpus*) was granted by law to publicani associations, which, among other functions, were responsible for tax collection. Later, commercial companies were able to benefit from legal personality, allowing them to be recognized as entities distinct from their members. Notably, the great royal companies, such as the East India Company, were constituted as joint-stock companies with a legal personality. However, for a long time, these companies required explicit Royal Charters or government authorization, which were granted sparingly and primarily for state-sanctioned operations.

The major breakthrough, which sparked virulent debates during the nineteenth century, was the liberalization of limited liability for corporations (which were endowed with legal personality). Under this system, none of the members was held personally liable with their own assets: all enjoyed limited liability (Djelic, 2013). This legal tool made it possible to raise substantial capital, typically for financing large infrastructure projects such as canals or roads. However, for a long time, it was considered extremely dangerous because it did not adequately protect creditors in cases of bankruptcy.

In France, for example, the Council of Mines advised at the beginning of the nineteenth century against authorizing the creation of corporations for activities involving exploration or innovation, which – as a result – did not provide sufficient guarantees to creditors regarding the sustainability of the business (Lefebvre-Teillard, 1985).

Nevertheless, with increasing industrialization at the end of the eighteenth and throughout the nineteenth centuries, the need to support business development pushed for the liberalization of corporations. This went hand in hand with the regulated authorization of bankruptcies. From the second half of the nineteenth century onwards, corporations were thus possible in the US and Europe, subject to a few conditions such as a minimum (publicly known) capital stock and the obligation to have an auditor (Lefebvre-Teillard, 1985).

3.1.2 Directors as Corporate Delegates

The general scheme of the business corporation has since remained relatively stable to this day. It can be summarized as follows (see Box 2): the members (or shareholders) share the profits and losses. Each share gives the right to participate in the AGM and have access to information, a right to vote, and a right to dividends. The AGM approves the financial statements and appoints (and if necessary revokes) its representatives who sit on the board of directors. Previously one had to be a shareholder to be a director; today the corporation's articles can freely define the minimum threshold necessary. The principle, therefore, is that the shareholders,

Box 2 The elements of the legal form of the corporation

Here are the main vital elements of the legal form of the corporation (Excerpted from Clarke, 2021, p. 4):

- **Limited Liability**: The losses an investor may bear are limited to the capital invested in the enterprise and do not extend to personal assets.
- **Transferability of Shares**: Shareholder rights may be transferred without constituting legal reorganization of the enterprise.
- **Juridical Personality:** The corporation itself becomes a fictive person, a legal entity that may sue or be sued, make contracts, and hold property.
- **Indefinite Duration:** The life of the corporation may extend beyond the participation of its original founders (and may continue indefinitely).

who can be very numerous, no longer directly manage the business themselves but entrust its administration to directors. Once appointed, directors must run the business not in their own interest, nor in the interest of specific members, but in the interest of the legal entity. And they can also delegate executive management to a general manager. The denomination of this general manager varies. In England, it has long been designated a "managing director" (Segrestin et al., 2019); in France, as early as 1867, it was indicated that the general manager could be a "foreigner" to the corporation, in other words, not a shareholder himself. The corporation's articles of association, beyond the imperative rules provided by law, have the force of law among the members: they govern the relations between the members and the directors. The corporation thus resembles for some a kind of republic of shareholders, with a private constitutional order (Ciepley, 2013; Grandori, 2022).

We will not go further in the description, albeit very brief, of the corporation. Nor will we go into the detail of the disparities between legislations here. For our discussion, remember that the legal framework of the corporation was – at its liberalization in the middle of the nineteenth century – perfectly in line with the standard economic representation: the shareholders are the capital providers. They decide together, or via their representatives, on the use of this capital, which will typically allow acquiring production means, and consequently share the profits (or losses) that these means of production will generate.

This representation sets out in a certain way the grammar that still remains dominant today: capital – via the corporation – grants a right of ownership over the means of production. The corporation mobilizes its means of production in exchange for remunerating workers and suppliers, to generate a profit that will ultimately be shared among the shareholders. However, this representation overlooks one radical and deep transformation in the nature of the activity that corporations experienced at the end of the nineteenth century and the birth of the managerial function needed to conceive and implement this activity.

3.2 The Rise of Modern Management: A New Creative Power

The advent of modern management occurred later than the development of corporate law (Segrestin et al., 2019). The first "business administration" programs opened at Harvard in 1908 (Khurana, 2007). It was only toward the very end of the nineteenth century that a growing distinction between the roles of board member and executive officer became apparent.

It is not our intention here to recount the history of modern and professional management. We merely wish to shed light on the conditions under which modern enterprises needed to both employ professional managers and recognize the subordination of employees: throughout the nineteenth century, workers were, in fact, independent. The old "master–servant relationships" had given way, in theory, to a contractual principle assuming both the autonomy and the equality of the parties (Selznick, 1969). The French Revolution, for instance, proscribed unequal relations. Workers had contracts of hire with their employer – which would today resemble commercial relationships between a client and a supplier. How then to understand the introduction – paradoxically perceived as a social advancement at the beginning of the twentieth century – of the labor law that enshrines the subordination of employees?

The birth of modern management can be explained by the profound transformation of the industrial activity regime at the end of the nineteenth century (Jacoby, 2004). At that time, there was a scientific and technical explosion and the emergence of a whole array of industries that could be described as science-based: chemistry, electrochemistry, electricity, and so on. Industrial organizations began to invest heavily in scientific research activities (Reich, 1985). The number of industrial research laboratories grew significantly, especially in the US. The most emblematic examples are well known: Bell Labs, AT&T, DuPont de Nemours, and ABB. The promises of scientific and industrial progress were considerable, and the wonders of industry were highly praised. Alongside research departments, there also emerged design offices and methods offices that systematized the development of new products and technologies. Companies transformed their organizations with the aim of "domesticating innovation" (Le Masson & Weil, 2008).

This evolution marks a shift in industrial activity. It is no longer merely productive but also inventive, creative. This has very deep implications on several levels.

3.2.1 Capabilities Building Rather Than Resources Exploitation

Firstly, the economic model changes. To put it simply, what constitutes the power of a company in regimes of intensive innovation is not the amount of capital held but the ability to find new value-creating uses for it. It is no longer the patent that one holds that counts but the company's capacity to file new patents, to develop new technologies. The example of Henri Fayol is illustrative. Henri Fayol is well known for his seminal book on business administration (Fayol, 1917). Fayol, one of the first managing directors to not be a shareholder or come from a shareholder family – he was a mere engineer – demonstrated this brilliantly in the steel company he managed from 1888 (Hatchuel & Segrestin, 2019). The shareholders had offered him the chief executive position when the company was in a significant crisis, asking him to sell or close the unprofitable mines and activities. But he defended that an asset has no value in itself. Fayol refused to close the unprofitable assets, considering that their profitability depended on how they were managed and what was done with them (Peaucelle, 2003). In this case, he created a research laboratory, which was extremely fruitful and from which, for example, patents for new alloys emerged. Invar, an alloy with a very low coefficient of expansion, was of considerable value for numerous applications, such as for watchmaking. Invar represented for several years a small volume of sales in terms of tons but a very significant part of the turnover. It illustrates well how management of a company's scientific and creative activities can overturn the classic economic analysis that sees the means of production as given sources of value.

3.2.2 Transformational Work

Secondly, the change in the regime of activity also transforms industrial relations. In a stable production regime, one can assume that the skills to ensure production are already present: the labor market can then function. Throughout the nineteenth century, workers could thus be paid on a piece-rate basis: by the ton of ore they brought back in the mines or by the piece in industries if they respected the specifications given to them. Workers operated with their own skills, their own methods, and often their own tools. They were therefore independent workers. However, as products change at an increasing rate and machinery develops, the innovation regime can no longer rely on the labor market. Taylor became known for denouncing piecework pay (Taylor, 1895): he observed incessant conflicts over negotiations on rates. But his analysis was that bargaining was of no use if workers did not have the proper methods or knowledge to perform the work effectively (Hatchuel, 1994). He showed in a famous experiment on metal cutting that optimizing metal cutting required mastering an experimental plan and knowing several sophisticated parameters, such as the nature of the sheet, the conditions of temperature and pressure, and so on. Hence the challenge for him to specialize the organization's actors in "shop management" (Taylor, 1911). The methods engineers will thus be responsible for developing – as products and techniques renew – the instructions and methods of work. From then on, the worker is no longer independent: they enter the company by agreeing to adopt the collective methods defined by management. And it is under these conditions that the necessity of recognizing subordination can be understood. Subordination was, in fact, a pledge of progress from the moment management was guided by a scientific approach that allowed escaping the sterile and violent confrontation between capital and labor. For Taylor, but it is too often forgotten, management had to be accompanied by guarantees toward employees and solidarity. Since productivity depended on management, workers could no longer be held responsible for low or poor production. They were to receive a guaranteed wage. And labor law went in this direction: Recognizing subordination was necessary to make hierarchical power more accountable. Managerial decisions had to be contestable and justifiable (Selznick, 1969). On the other hand, it can be noted that labor law did not go all the way and did not recognize the real effects of subordination. Because with the innovative regime of activity and subordination, the very nature of work changes. Work, with the prescriptions of management, is indeed transformative: workers will develop skills, networks, and employability that no longer depend only on them but partly on management. In other words, where traditionally it is considered that capital investors assume the economic risk and that workers do not take risks since they receive a contractually fixed salary, it must be recognized that work transforms individuals' potential: their potential is at risk in the same way as investors' assets are at risk from the moment it is managed not by themselves but by a management team (Segrestin et al., 2020).

Overall, the transformation of industrial activity that is no longer merely productive but also creative relies on the emergence of a novel figure in economic history: that of the manager or executive officer. How to think of this new function, which at the beginning of the twentieth century puzzled observers like Berle and Means who hesitated whether to see this as a new "dictator" or a "neutral technocracy" (Berle & Means, [1932] 1991)?

3.2.3 Managerial Authority

If we think of management as the function that designs and implements new forms of collective action (making inventive use of resources to create wealth), then management should not be solely defined by its capacity for hierarchical command. We can outline a few conditions that managerial authority would need to meet to be both effective and legitimate (Segrestin & Hatchuel, 2011).

First, managers should be creative and would therefore need distinctive skills. Second, they should be able to mobilize and inspire trust, bringing various stakeholders on board for unprecedented ventures with uncertain outcomes. This would require acting with caution and responsibility, as well as being accountable for the consequences of these ventures. As a prerequisite, this would also demand specific skills: in particular, managers should be able to identify risks, manage them effectively, and keep them under control. The cognitive dimensions of this role should therefore not be underestimated (Grandori, 2001a, 2001b, 2022; Grandori & Furlotti, 2019).

Finally, if leaders are to be chosen for their creative talent and competence in risk management, they should be granted the necessary leeway to exercise judgment and make decisions, free from undue pressure or incentives from various stakeholders.

3.3 The Inappropriate Status of Management in Corporate Law

Yet, neither managerial discretion nor managerial responsibility is fully recognized in corporate law (Segrestin et al., 2019). Ultimately, it must be acknowledged that the status of the business leader is eminently problematic in law.

3.3.1 The Chief Executive: Agent or Discretionary Power?

First, the legal status of managers is somewhat contradictory: the authority of the executives is at the heart of labor law, but it is not recognized in corporate law. Labor law is actually founded on the recognition of the power to manage: this implies some conditions. The underlying principle is one of protecting subordinates, but also the responsibility of the person exercising managerial power. In our view, the best illustration of this responsibility comes from workplace accidents (Hatchuel & Segrestin, 2020). The law on workplace accidents laid the first foundations for what would become labor law in Europe and the United States (Commons, 1919). It represents a law profoundly derogatory to the normal regime of responsibility. Normally, one is responsible only for one's own faults. In the case of workplace accidents, with this law, the employer is deemed responsible for the employee's accident, even if the employee is at fault or has not followed instructions. This may seem paradoxical, but the law is fully justified: on one hand, the employer organizes work. It is therefore his or her responsibility to ensure that the production processes they design and implement are safe. This implies a particular competence. In other words, being a manager implies being competent in safety and security and refraining from ordering work from employees that is not assured to be safe. On the other hand, the employer is responsible, but it can be a responsibility without fault: if all precautions have been taken and the work processes are indeed secure, accidents can still occur. This is the theory of "objective" industrial risk that prevailed during parliamentary debates in France at the end of the nineteenth century (Saleilles, 1897). Hence the idea that the employer can be insured against this risk, and must even be insured to be able to compensate the victims of workplace accidents. But insurance, as we see, can play its role only if the manager has acted responsibly, and the work protocols did not expose any employee to undue risks. This example shows how the power to direct necessarily goes hand in hand with both a requirement for specific managerial competence and a clear social responsibility, which could be described as a duty of vigilance regarding the risks induced by the activity organized by the management.

However, if labor law is built on the recognition and responsibility of the CEO, corporate law is nothing of the sort. In corporate law, the executive officer is an individual to whom the board of directors has delegated the executive management of operations. The board actually retains responsibility for the strategy and its execution. The CEO is thus a sort of corporate delegate, endowed with extensive powers to represent the company and engage it in relations with third parties, but always under the high responsibility of the board of directors. The board of directors can at any time withdraw its confidence and revoke him. Thus, following corporate law, it is understandable that economists have assimilated the managerial function to that of an agent: in corporate law, it is an agent who acts in the name and on behalf of the board of directors, whose members are themselves appointed by the shareholders.[4] Corporate law does not recognize either the power to direct or the responsibilities associated with managing operations that could involve risks for third parties. Thus, by the end of the twentieth century, the chief executive is in charge of running activities with a now global and considerable impact on a number of resources and parties other than the corporate shareholders; but on the other side, he/she is accountable only before the board of directors, who are themselves appointed by shareholders.

3.3.2 An Unfounded Authority

The power to manage of the business leader is also of little legitimacy insofar as its foundation remains eminently problematic. What can justify a private power

[4] Many authors remind us that directors in several jurisdictions, particularly in the United States, benefit from the "business judgment rule" (BJR). This rule grants directors significant latitude, as their decisions cannot, in principle, be contested in court (except in cases of disloyalty or gross negligence). Directors, therefore, have in law an important discretion, although in practice this is limited – particularly by incentives and theoretical frameworks that view the role of management as serving shareholders (Sjåfjell et al., 2015).

over subordinated employees within a company when all individuals are equal citizens in the city? This question far exceeds the scope of this Element. Nevertheless, it is important to measure again the problematic nature of the inherited corporate law. How to justify this power to manage? Following the analysis of Selznick, we can review several classical hypotheses (Selznick, 1969). The idea that it stems from the property right is untenable. Ownership of a thing cannot confer the power to direct people who use that thing (McMahon, 2013). And the company, while it may own assets, cannot own individuals. Similarly, the concept of the corporation, as a separate legal person, has sometimes been advanced to justify a shared authority. But if the corporation cannot be reduced to the aggregation of its members alone, as Selznick aptly shows, it does not grant any rights, particularly not control rights, to other parties. The possibility remains to consider that the authority is consented to by contract between the employee and the employer. But the attributes of a contract, notably the condition of autonomy of will of the parties, do not align well with the nature of relationships within the company. Selznick analyzes the emergence of the employment contract as a mode of submission, entrenching prerogatives for the employer under the guise of false contractualism. Master–servant relationships have been abolished in favor of "truly contractual employment relationships," but in reality the employment contract is a "prerogative contract." Paradoxically, contractual theory authorized a form of sovereign and absolute authority of managers because they were not bound by rules beyond breaking the contract. The contract presupposes relations between equals, but in reality the law has maintained the employer's prerogatives: "[t]he result was a marriage of old master-servant notions to an apparently uncompromising contractualism" (Selznick, 1969, p. 136).

Another justification, however, remains regularly advanced today: the authority would be consented to by individuals as long as they recognize that cooperation requires a coordinator or an orchestrator. This was the thesis of F. Knight at the beginning of the twentieth century: according to him, the more a collective endeavor moves into uncertainty or the unknown, the more its members need to rely on management authority (Knight, 1921). The options and their consequences are indeed not known and not evaluable by the different actors. Under these conditions, it is necessary to rely on the one who is considered the most capable of exercising judgment. More recently, this position has been taken up by theorists of cooperation (Lopes, 2022). It is of course relevant, but it does not answer all the questions. In particular, it overlooks the question of the conditions under which cooperation can be desirable for individuals. Isn't cooperation, and therefore authority, desirable only insofar as it effectively aims at the interest of its members? Authority presupposes being able to speak in a "common name" (Hauriou, 1899). This actually underlines not a justification but a fundamental condition of the legitimacy of authority: authority can be exercised only in the interest of those over whom it is exercised (McMahon, 2013). But how can this interest be defined, especially if the authority is transformative? It is not trivial to emphasize that among the first theorists of the function of the executives, Barnard considered that the main of the responsibilities of the leader was to define a "common purpose" of the organization, that is to say, a purpose that specifically aims to reconcile the common objective of the organization with the interests of all the members that the organization involves (Barnard, [1938] 1968). This responsibility is remarkably absent from corporate law.

The authority of the business manager is therefore not established in corporate law; moreover, the necessary conditions – competence, discretion, and the responsibility to pursue a 'common purpose' – for the manager to exercise their authority legitimately are not explicitly stated. This gap in a way opened the door, from the 1970s onwards, to the excesses of shareholder governance and a profound crisis in the corporation. On the corporate law side, executives, supervised by shareholders, were pressured to implement policies that ensured a return on investment for the shareholders, thereby ignoring their responsibilities as leaders and managerial authorities, even if this meant jeopardizing the future of the company by cutting back on investment in research and development (Arora et al., 2018) or by dismantling the interdependent activities of the company (Lazonick, 2023).

3.4 The Different Paths to Conceptualizing Management

Numerous efforts to propose conceptualizations of management and its responsibility have been made. Several concepts have been advanced that seek to reconcile, on one hand, the legal framework of the corporation and, on the other hand, the necessary leeway of management decision-making. We briefly present in Sections 3.4.1–3.4.4 the most prominent concepts, before questioning their feedback effect on corporate law.

3.4.1 Managers as Trustees or Fiduciaries

The first concept is that of trusteeship, and it was used to describe directors, rather than managers, in a context where both were conceptually hard to differentiate. Berle refers to this notion in 1931 to question the power of direction in reference to trust law (Berle Jr., 1931). A trust is a legal act by which an individual (or a legal entity) – the settlor – transfers assets to a person – the trustee – who will then have the responsibility of managing them on behalf of one or more designated beneficiaries. Unlike corporate law, the legal framework of the trust therefore forces one to specify who the beneficiary of the trust is and thus what the purpose is. Berle clearly uses this reference to provoke a clarification of expectations toward directors, and consequently their responsibilities.

Dodd's response, as we know, in this well-known debate we have already mentioned, will be significant: the director is the trustee not of the associates or such stakeholders but of the corporation itself (Dodd, 1932). Since then, this idea is often reiterated, further emphasizing that directors are "autonomous fiduciaries." Lan and Heracleous thus wrote in 2010 an article that denounces the unfounded nature of agency theory (Lan & Heracleous, 2010). And they write:

> The director primacy model positions directors as autonomous fiduciaries, not agents (Clark, 1985; Ferran, 1999). In law, a fiduciary individual is someone who is entrusted with the power to act on behalf of and for the benefit of another. The term fiduciary derives from the Latin fiducia, or trust, and the fiduciary is expected to act in good faith and honesty for the beneficiary's interests. A person who accepts the role of fiduciary in law must single-mindedly pursue the interests of his or her beneficiary, in this case the corporation (Model Business Corporation Act § 8.30), even when the latter cannot monitor or control the fiduciary's behavior (Blair & Stout, 2001 []; Clark, 1985)." (Lan & Heracleous, 2010, p. 302)

Another concept, quite similar, with which to characterize the role of the board is that of "mediating hierarch." The idea, advanced notably by Blair and Stout (1999), is that the role of the board is to ensure that the different parties are justly compensated so that they agree to get involved in the enterprise despite uncertainties about the returns they can derive from it. The creation of a legal entity, the corporation, owner of the assets and results, would thus be a means to avoid endless negotiations between the parties and to ensure everyone a fair return. Here, it is less the role of the manager that is considered than that of the board of directors. In Blair and Stout's view, the manager is a member of the team like the others, a "bona fide team member" who simply has a particular competence and coordination role. And, again, it is assumed that the board has sufficient latitude of action to ensure a role as a mediator independently of the shareholders' exclusive control rights – an assumption that, as we have seen, is now difficult to maintain.

3.4.2 Stakeholder Management

It is toward management research that we must turn to better grasp the figure of the manager as a responsible authority, particularly with the notion of "stakeholder management." This notion was popularized by Freeman (1988) in the 1980s. For Freeman, the idea that business aims to maximize shareholder value is outdated and a source of crises. The challenge is to dedicate the management of stakeholders: the role of management is to create value for the different stakeholders without resorting to trade-offs. In this approach, companies thrive because they manage to align the interests of stakeholders with each other (Donaldson & Preston, 1995).

Nevertheless, the stakeholder approach does not go as far as to question the law or the imbalance within the governance bodies between associates and other parties. The stakeholder theory has mainly developed in an instrumental logic. It does not challenge the fact that, in the end, the role of managers is indeed to serve the economic efficiency of the company, and its financial performance (Margolis & Walsh, 2003). As long as shareholders bear the risks and are paid as a last resort, profit can indicate that all parties have been treated and remunerated fairly. However, as previously mentioned, shareholders' exclusive control rights can lead to transferring risks onto other parties and securing profit without prosperity (Lazonick, 2014). In 2002, the movement took a step further by seeking an institutional translation of the principles of stakeholder management to counterbalance the principles of corporate governance for managers. The "Clarkson principles" thus stipulate that managers should:

- [Principle 1] acknowledge and actively monitor the concerns of all legitimate stakeholders, and . . . take their interests appropriately into account in decision-making and operations;
- and [Principle 2] . . . listen to and openly communicate with stakeholders about their respective concerns and contributions, and about the risks that they assume because of their involvement with the corporation.

The initiative remains presented from an instrumental point of view: according to Donaldson, one of the most recognized professors in the field, the Clarkson principles are based on "a growing conviction among many participating scholars that mutually satisfactory relationships with a wide range of stakeholders are a critical requirement for successful corporate performance over the long term" (Donaldson, 2002, p. 108).

3.4.3 Managers as Stewards

In the 1990s, the psychological posture of the executives and the assumptions of opportunism were discussed. Managers were presented as "stewards" rather than "agents," meaning individuals who genuinely seek the success of the collective rather than their own particular interests. Where the opportunistic agent is naturally driven by self-interest, the steward is motivated primarily by the success of the collective enterprise and puts personal interest in the background (Davis et al., 1997; Donaldson & Davis, 1991; Hernandez, 2012). This literature has had a significant impact because it offers theoretical lenses that are consistent with numerous empirical observations. However, it also emphasizes that this psychological orientation is dependent on the orientation of the trustees and is therefore necessarily fragile (Davis et al., 1997).

3.4.4 Managers as Professionals

Beyond psychological orientation, the literature has also focused on the competencies and methods of management to justify the necessity of a degree of discretion left by shareholders to managers. In a way, given the knowledge – often changing and complex – required for the managerial function, leaders cannot be controlled by shareholders (Sharma, 1997), but should rather be perceived as professionals (Khurana, 2007). And as professionals, with the authority of the science upon which their knowledge is based, they would have an ethos oriented toward the common interest and a duty toward the community. This was, at least, the conviction and ambition of the first business schools that sought to develop the scientific dimension of management and the character of management as a progressive rationalizer in times when conflicts often opposed labor and capital (Khurana, 2007). "Managers are professionals because they possess specialized coordination skills that are markedly different from those of businesspersons" (Kaufman, 2002). And the empirical reality of technocracy is hardly in doubt (Galbraith, [1967] 1989).

Nevertheless, as is known, this ambition from the 1950s and 1960s was soon caught up by other logics, notably corporatist ones, and led to the discrediting of the institutions that upheld it. The idea of an uncontrolled technocracy was in reality all the more questionable and dubious as it did not clearly qualify the common interest it was supposed to serve. Under these circumstances, agency theory in the 1970s and 1980s was particularly influential in asserting that executives needed to be more controlled and that their role was primarily to serve the mandates of their principals, that is, their shareholders.

This brief journey through the different conceptualizations of management leads us to a simple conclusion: There have been numerous attempts to conceive of the role of management as responsible and capable of taking into account the social and environmental issues of the activity. Nevertheless, these various conceptualizations most often did not question the framework of corporate law. They attempted to act as if corporate law allowed leeway for management decision-making and the pursuit of purposes different from the private interest of the shareholders. But today, this hypothesis, as we have shown here, is becoming difficult to uphold. And the ambivalence of corporate law or even the lack of conceptualization in law of the conditions in which management can be legitimate is becoming increasingly untenable.

3.5 Incorporating Purpose: Towards New Legal Foundations for Responsible Management

Today, the impact of management decisions affects not only employees but entire populations and even the planet. Managers of companies like Google and Amazon, as well as smaller entities like OpenAI, have a clearly decisive influence on the world. Similarly, managers of companies expanding oil exploration, or those developing CO_2 capture solutions, also have a significant capacity to act on the future of the planet. Size and financial capital or revenue are far from the only variables. It is more fundamentally because the enterprise is capable of research and innovation that it has become a transformative or transformational power in the world. As Colin Mayer eloquently puts it:[5]

> I'm going to talk to you about the most or one of the most important institutions in our lives. I'm not talking about the state, religion, or the Kennedy School. I'm talking to you about an institution that clothes, feeds, and houses us, employs us and invests our savings. It's a source of economic prosperity and the growth of nations around the world. At the same time, it could be a source of bringing inequality, environmental degradation, and mistrust. (Mayer, 2019, p. 2)

Business companies have a massive transformational power. For better, one might say, for worse. We owe to enterprises some of the most beneficial innovations to humanity. But we also owe to businesses major social and ecological imbalances. Especially today, businesses are investing in fields of activity where we know that the implications will be radical for our societies and our ways of life, as for the habitability of the planet, but we cannot say a priori if they will be beneficial or not. The field of artificial intelligence is symptomatic of this fundamental uncertainty, in the face of which states are quite powerless. But it is far from the only one; the life sciences contain just as much unknown, that is, parts of hopes and major risks.

To put it simply, since the birth of modern management, businesses have acquired a transformative power in the world that goes well beyond what labor

[5] "The purpose and future of the corporation," a speech given by Colin Mayer, CBE, former Dean of Said Business School, Oxford University, on February 21, 2019, as part of the Mossavar-Rahmani Center for Business and Government at the Harvard Kennedy School's weekly Business and Government Seminar Series (Mayer 2019).

law can regulate. Decision-making of corporate leaders involves resources that go far beyond those of the corporate members. But also today, far beyond just employees. It involves territories, the environment, and society as a whole – modes of communication, relationships between individuals. In short, it can be said that management decisions now touch all aspects of the human condition: societal, cultural, scientific, ecological, anthropological . . . (Levillain et al., 2020).

Yet, the decision power of management is still governed today by corporate law, even if corporate law was set up even before the birth of modern management. Management decisions can be subject to various professional rules (such as codes of ethics or prudence in finance), environmental laws, or other branches of law. But in corporate law, managers always run the company on behalf of and under the responsibility of directors. In corporate law, the rationality of management decisions is therefore ultimately supervised by shareholders. And it may be considered good management to seek to circumvent fiscal, social, and environmental obligations – as long as it remains within the bounds of legality – if it increases shareholders' interests. This mismatch between the potential impact of management and the corporate framework that governs it cannot be underestimated.

It becomes urgent today to rethink the legal conditions for responsible management. This involves defining under what conditions management decisions are legitimate – or, conversely, under what conditions they constitute misconduct, independently of shareholders' expectations.

In the rest of this section, we would like to show that this movement is already underway. There are two complementary areas where corporate law is evolving to define the conditions for legitimate and responsible management:

- On one hand, the duty of vigilance was introduced in France in 2017 and extended at the European level with the Due Diligence Directive in 2024: it establishes a corporate obligation for management to map risks to fundamental rights induced by the activity and ensure that these risks are controlled. This duty extends risk management principles beyond workplace safety.
- On the other hand, the law introduces corporate forms that constitutionalize a purpose with social and environmental objectives: such a purpose sets the conditions that must be respected in the management of future activities, regardless of shareholders' expectations. By designating a future of collective interest, the purpose can establish the foundations of managerial legitimacy, while also introducing a new principle of managerial accountability.

As we will see in Section 4, the emerging forms of purpose-driven corporations are very heterogeneous in how they define their purpose, as well as in how they organize – or do not organize – its oversight and the contestability of management decisions. For now, however, we focus on the potential of the purpose to serve as a legal foundation for management in corporate law.

3.5.1 A Duty of Due Diligence with Respect to Fundamental Rights and the Environment

It is no longer only work safety risks that managers must control, but more generally all risks of serious harm to fundamental human rights and the environment. Such a duty of vigilance was established in France in 2017 (Hatchuel & Segrestin, 2020). It requires all large ordering companies to establish a risk management plan throughout their value chain (see Box 3). The reasoning that was held in terms of work accidents at the end of the nineteenth century is here expanded: the management of a company thinks of a strategy that assumes the mobilization of various resources, with multiple subcontracting relationships. But such organizational power is acceptable only if management is competent regarding the risks induced along the value chain. And it must be able to organize itself to ensure that work can be made safe. It is therefore its responsibility to eliminate risks that are foreseeable – within the state of the art or the knowledge of the expert – and to renounce activities that may cause unmanageable risks. The duty of vigilance thus introduces an obligation for large companies to establish a risk management plan for breaches of fundamental rights, even if these risks are outside the company's perimeter of liability, notably those that appear with suppliers. Indeed, a company is not liable for the actions of its suppliers who are legally autonomous persons. Nonetheless, being in charge of managing the activity implies being able to assess the risks. A leader can therefore be held accountable not for the poor management of its suppliers but rather for not having established a quality risk management plan and for not having been able to avoid risks that were avoidable. A similar duty of due diligence was introduced at the European level in the Corporate Sustainability

Box 3 Due diligence – duty of vigilance in the French law of 2017 – excerpt

Article L225-102-4.-I. Every company ... establishes and effectively implements a vigilance plan. ...

The plan includes reasonable vigilance measures aimed at identifying risks and preventing serious harm to human rights and fundamental freedoms, the health and safety of individuals, and the environment, resulting from the company's activities and those of the companies it controls within the meaning of paragraph II of Article L233-16, directly or indirectly, as well as the activities of subcontractors or suppliers with

Box 3 (cont.)

whom an established commercial relationship is maintained, when these activities are linked to this relationship.

It includes the following measures:

1° A risk mapping aimed at their identification, analysis, and prioritization;
2° Procedures for regular assessment of the situation of subsidiaries, subcontractors, or suppliers with whom an established commercial relationship is maintained, in light of the risk mapping;
3° Appropriate actions to mitigate risks or prevent serious harm;
4° An alert mechanism and collection of reports related to the existence or realization of risks, established in consultation with the representative trade unions in the said company;
5° A system for monitoring the measures implemented and assessing their effectiveness.

The vigilance plan and the report on its effective implementation are made public and included in the report referred to in Article L225-102.

Due Diligence Directive (CSDDD) in 2024. It includes the notion of environmental harm and risks of noncompliance with the Paris Agreement (Ventura, 2023).

3.5.2 Purpose: The Expression of the Conditions for Responsible Management

The duty of due diligence requires management decisions to take into account known or foreseeable risks to fundamental rights. But today, the challenge is to more broadly hold management decisions accountable for the futures they help create.

This is where the legal concept of "purpose" can play a particularly important role in re-founding management and the corporation. We do not claim that it is the only means or that it solves all problems. However, introducing a purpose into the company's constitution seems to us a promising way to overcome the current gap between the world-transforming power of management, on the one hand, and corporate law where management is accountable only to shareholders, on the other.

Several arguments support this view.

3.5.2.1 Aligning Corporate Governance and Management Authority

Currently, the role of chief executives has two inconsistent facets: on the side of the enterprise, the manager is an authority figure who must be able to mobilize various stakeholders and take their respective interests into account. On the side of corporate governance, however, the manager no longer holds authority but is instead regarded as an 'agent' under control, tasked with running the business on behalf of the shareholders.

Incorporating a purpose into the corporate constitution can restore coherence between these two facets. First, if the purpose encompasses the company's activity (e.g., bringing potable water to certain regions, developing safe artificial intelligence tools, etc.), it can bring sustainability issues and non-shareholder stakeholders into the core of corporate governance. This broadens the scope of what corporate leaders must address. Consequently, the company's interest can no longer be reduced to that of its shareholders once the purpose includes considerations related to the sustainability of its activities. Next, it establishes objectives that commits the corporation beyond shareholders' expectations. In this way, it has the potential to protect managerial leeway. And if it truly corresponds to a 'common purpose' (Barnard, [1938] 1968), then the purpose also has the capacity to legitimize managerial authority. Finally, the purpose can foster a new form of accountability for management: this necessitates control and monitoring mechanisms, which we will explore further in Section 4.

3.5.2.2 Acknowledging a Creative Function

The elucidation of the purpose – the ends that can be aspirational, like the development of environmental technologies or the fight against inequalities in a territory – should not lead to denying potential difficulties. The solutions are not given in advance. And leaders will always have to manage different expectations, and sometimes manage strong antagonisms between profit expectations and the other dimensions of the broader purpose. But in a way, it is these tensions that justify the recourse to management and a form of management authority. If the solution were known a priori, then perhaps simpler contractual relationships would be preferable to that of a management authority. The purpose explicates the creative function of management.

3.5.2.3 Aligning Responsibility with Corporate Creative Power

Finally, purpose lays the groundwork for a form of responsibility suited to the enterprise of collective creation. Traditionally, a company is legally responsible for the harm its activities cause to its surroundings. However, when a company is creative, it has the potential to transform the world of tomorrow, and its impact extends beyond its current stakeholders. If a purpose articulates the sustainable future the company aims to build, incorporating that purpose into the corporate constitution establishes a foundation for holding the company accountable—not only for the immediate harm it may cause but also for the activities it undertakes today that will shape the world of tomorrow.

3.6 Section Conclusion: Key Elements

In summary, corporate law was liberalized during the nineteenth century before the birth of modern management. With it, the governance structure of the classic corporation stabilized. Shareholders are at the origin of the creation of a company. They appoint and dismiss directors and share the profits, or losses if necessary. In this framework, the activity is not necessarily mentioned, and stakeholders other than shareholders are legally third parties.

However, after corporate law was stabilized, the managerial function appeared in a context of profound transformation of the nature of the activity. The activity increasingly included research and innovation, which required the intervention of a management authority capable of both proposing a novel collective strategy and implementing it. Such creative authority, engaging various parties in ventures with unknown consequences, implies that leaders must possess distinctive skills, genuine latitude for action, and accountability for the impacts of their decisions. Nevertheless, attempts to conceptualize the management function sought to inculcate principles of responsibility or ethics in management without changing the legal framework of corporate governance.

There is a strong mismatch today between the impact that the management of business activities can have and the way management is governed, that is, nominated, compensated, and supervised in corporate law.

In some countries, corporate law has started to establish new legal foundations for responsible management, beyond the expectations of the shareholders, at two levels: On the one hand, the duty of due diligence imposes a principle of vigilant management with regard to fundamental rights. On the other hand, corporate law can invite companies to explicitly state, through a binding constitutional purpose, the conditions under which management decisions will be considered legitimate and responsible. If the purpose defines the sustainable future the corporation aims to create and truly corresponds to a 'common purpose,' it establishes the managerial function within the corporation, moves beyond the notion that managers are merely agents, and grounds the legitimacy of their authority. It also serves as a basis for management accountability, as it allows for the possibility of challenging – potentially in court – management decisions that fail to comply with the purpose. While the theoretical principle has significant potential, it remains to be seen how the purpose is defined in practice and, more importantly, what governance structures are in place to effectively oversee and enforce it. This is what we will explore in Section 4.

4 Purpose-Driven Corporations: A Renewed Landscape of Alternative Governance Structures

For several years now, many states have adopted new forms of corporations to pursue a purpose that is broader and beyond the mere maximization of profit. These new forms come in addition to the traditional legal forms, such as partnerships and corporations, as well as historical alternative corporate architectures, for example cooperatives. Such a renewal can only be welcomed, as corporate law has, for several decades, been considered an unquestioned given. This renewal reflects both the growing expectations of entrepreneurs and the vitality of reflections on corporate governance structures. Conversely, it is useful to take a step back and identify some landmarks with which to navigate this highly dynamic landscape.

The literature has shown that organizations pursuing a social goal in addition to profit traditionally face two unsatisfactory alternatives (Battilana et al., 2012): on one hand, the for-profit corporation and, on the other, the nonprofit association. Such a duality has been reinforced, as we have seen, by theoretical approaches that have reduced the purpose of the corporation solely to profit. Today, it is even more imperative to move beyond this classic divide as the challenges of ecological transitions demand that companies not only manage their negative impacts but also contribute to these transitions. However, there are other possible options beyond the nonprofit association or the primarily for-profit corporation. The question is whether and under what conditions the legal governance structures allow for varied purposes, broader than mere profit: how can governance structures secure and protect these different purposes over time? And also, how can they make them credible, controllable, and enforceable?

In this Element, by governance structures we mean the way in which the company distributes rights and responsibilities among its stakeholders (Aguilera & Jackson, 2003). The governance structure, whether it is invented and adopted by a company at the local level or proposed by law at the national level, always has legal effects: it binds the parties to one another. And if its rules are not respected, it can lead to legal action in the courts.

In this section, we discuss alternative corporate forms, or alternative "ways of organizing,"[6] through the lens of purpose. The lens of purpose invites us to examine governance structures from two perspectives:

[6] Mair and Rathert (2021, p. 819) define "alternative way of organizing" as "market-based activity with a social purpose carried out by a variety of organizational types": "Alternative forms of organizing diverge from 'the corporation' i.e. from what has been considered the organizational archetype [with a central objective of maximizing economic profits] in markets for much of the 20th century."

- **What purpose is being pursued?** Does it aim to uphold ethical or professional standards, defend particular causes, or promote disruption and innovation to bring about desirable futures? And is this purpose consistent with contemporary sustainability challenges?
- **To what extent is the purpose protected and enforceable?** In other words, to what extent do governance structures ensure the credibility and robustness of the purpose over time? This can be discussed at two levels: First, to what extent is the company legally bound by the purpose? There may be different lock-in mechanisms, some more or less subject to revision, for example. Second, what control and accountability mechanisms ensure the enforcement of the purpose? These mechanisms are evidently very heterogeneous, yet they determine the effectiveness and credibility of the purpose.

Our objective is twofold. First, we aim to situate the emergence of new legal forms of purpose-driven corporations within the broader landscape of alternative ways of organizing (Luyckx et al., 2022; Mair & Rathert, 2021). The general principle of a constitutional purpose allows for a rereading of historical alternative forms, by highlighting their purpose (or "primary organizing goals" [Mair & Rathert, 2021]) and discussing their governance structures as mechanisms for control and enforceability. We will only outline the discussion, which will warrant further in-depth analysis.

Second, among the variety of emerging legal frameworks for purpose-driven corporations, we wish to discuss in particular two new forms: the US benefit corporation and the French *société à mission*. Both of these legal forms are purpose-driven corporations, but, as we will see, they provide different models. The benefit corporation pursues a generic purpose without changing governance structures *per se* but with a requirement for disclosure and reporting. Conversely, the *société à mission* pursues a purpose specific to the company and requires a renewed governance structure to oversee management choices.

This section is not intended to be a guide or even a legal manual, which would require skills we do not possess and, more importantly, meticulous work according to legislation. Legislative contexts and legal cultures are very heterogeneous, and comparative law requires strong precautions. We will discuss mainly "archetypes" of legal forms, or situated examples. Above all, the goal is to highlight the space of conceptual alternatives that is emerging today in terms of legal frameworks and to enable an informed debate around these alternatives. Such a debate should interest both companies, for whom the space of choices is now reopened, and states, which now have the opportunity to promote more responsible enterprises.

4.1 Alternative Governance Structures through the Lens of the Purpose

4.1.1 Cooperatives

The most classic historical alternative to the for-profit corporation is the cooperative. The cooperative was born in the nineteenth century in the wake of significant social movements of various kinds (Schneiberg, 2011, 2013). It is now established worldwide. The principles that structure the cooperative are codified by the International Cooperative Alliance. Here we are more specifically interested in employee cooperatives insofar as our work focuses on the legal forms of the enterprise. However, cooperatives are also highly developed in different sectors, such as agricultural cooperatives.

The purpose of the cooperative is rather clear: it serves the members' need, and beyond that their economic and political emancipation. Before discussing such a purpose in the contemporary context, it is important to highlight how governance structures ensure the stability of, respect for, and alignment with the purpose. Employee cooperatives can use a classical form of company, typically the corporation; but they have additional rules in their constitution. Typically, and even though the modalities vary from one country to another, employees must hold the majority of the share capital. They thus control the company even if some cooperatives can welcome non-employee investors. In addition, the cooperative adopts a democratic principle whereby one member equals one vote. Such a principle breaks with the idea that shareholders have a voting weight corresponding to the capital they contribute and therefore to the risks they take. Finally, another important rule concerns the distribution of profits: the remuneration of work takes precedence over that of capital and, above all, the profits must systematically contribute to an indivisible reserve. This contributes to making the enterprise robust and less dependent on external capital contributions.

The form of the cooperative enterprise is ancient and persistent, even if it concerns relatively few companies overall. It has developed especially in sectors where employees are professionals who seek to share a common framework. It is nonetheless particularly interesting in that it has historically built a framework where employees are *legally* integrated into the company. Where in the classical enterprise there is a clear-cut distinction between the question of organizing activities, which typically falls under labor law, and that of governance, which falls under corporate law, the cooperative organizes a kind of unique coupling or symbiosis between the organization of work and corporate governance. It deserves our full attention for this reason.

At this point, a remark is necessary regarding the status of managers in cooperatives. The fact that employees participate in the designation of their leaders undoubtedly supports the latter's legitimacy. But beyond the fact that employees can democratically designate their leaders, the status of management is not so much clarified by the legal statutes of cooperatives. Indeed, by making employees their own shareholders, and therefore also the directors' electors, cooperatives have further pushed the idea that employees manage the company themselves in a form of democratic comanagement of the company. The status of management, capable of inventing a new strategy and orchestrating it, remains quite distant from cooperative functioning, even if in practice cooperatives can recruit professional managers whose authority is unquestionable. But the cooperative model, where employees are subordinates during the day and directors in the evening (Gide, 1924), does not help to clarify the status of management and its responsibilities.

If we now return to the question of the content of the purpose, the primary purpose of cooperatives is to serve its members to contribute to their emancipation and fulfillment. In doing so, it remains potentially disconnected from the nature of the activity. Like in a classical company, it is actually silent about the impacts that the activity can have on other stakeholders, and particularly on the environment. One of the essential issues for research, in our view, is to see to what extent cooperatives could pursue multiple purposes and – alongside the interest of the members – commit to ensuring that their activities are managed responsibly, or even to pursuing specific objectives (for example, environmental goals).

4.1.2 Codetermination

Another historical case where labor law and corporate law are interestingly coupled is that of codetermination, which prevails in Germany and most Nordic countries (Nyland et al., 2014).

Taking Germany as an example, companies with more than 2,000 employees have a supervisory board instead of a board of directors: this supervisory board is not in charge of defining strategy but rather of appointing the directors (the executive board) and overseeing them. However, this board is composed equally of shareholder representatives and employee representatives (only a third of employees for smaller companies between 500 and 2,000 employees).

Regarding the content, the same observation could potentially be made about codetermination as about the cooperative: the governance structure does not specify how management should address the potential impacts of the activity on other stakeholders and the environment. Nevertheless, the configuration is very different from that of the cooperative regarding the status of management.

German law indeed defines the purpose as the mandate given to the management board (Leixnering et al., 2022). According to the law (Aktiengesetz, § 76[1]), "The management board is responsible for managing the company independently. In doing so, it is bound to the well-being of the company, which also includes the interests of the shareholders, the employees, and the general public."

Regarding the governance structures, the question is to what extent they actually enforce this purpose. The supervisory board brings together employees and shareholders to supervise the management. Here, employees do not need to be shareholders themselves to participate in governance bodies. This model has been heavily criticized in shareholder-driven countries, but also in Southern European countries: they feared, in particular, that employee participation would block strategic orientations or that parity on the supervisory board would foster conflicts. In some ways, unions in these countries also pushed for a defense of employees from the outside and in opposition to management, not from within governance bodies. Yet this is where this model can be interesting. Some see it as a model of "stakeholder-agency," with leaders being simultaneously delegated by shareholders and employees (Asher et al., 2005). Alternatively, it can be hypothesized that it is the needed latitude – and authority – that managers have to manage both the capital of shareholders and the potential of employees, which explains this model: both parties have a right of oversight precisely because they renounce managing themselves and jointly accept management authority.

This hypothesis is worth exploring. In any case, the codetermination model invites us to question the status of the manager, who can no longer be simply equated to an agent who manages affairs on behalf of and for the account of corporate members.

4.1.3 Shareholder Foundation

The governance structure by a shareholder foundation is not – to our knowledge – a specific legal form of enterprise institutionalized by law. It is rather an invention by practice, with companies historically seizing the legal instrument of the foundation to change their governance structure. Nevertheless, it is now a fairly widespread invention in certain countries (Germany and the Nordic countries, in particular) (Ciepley, 2018; Thomsen et al., 2018). And it has the great merit, for our purposes, of dedicating for the first time a specific purpose within the governance structure of the company.

To present it, let's take the historical case of Carl Zeiss, who, so to speak, invented the first form of a purpose-driven corporation ahead of its time (Goyder, 1951, 1987; Segrestin, 2017). Zeiss created his optical instruments workshop in 1846 in Germany (Jena). His business prospered, but it became especially successful when he poached a professor, Ernst Abbe, from the university. He scientifically modeled the behaviors of light rays and allowed considerable progress in optical instruments. Until then, an optical lens had to be worked through long and complicated adjustments to obtain an undistorted image. By explaining how impurities could divert the rays, Abbe was able to define the geometry of the glass surface to be machined, and he greatly facilitated the development of microscopes. Such progress, with all the applications it implies, for example in medicine, illustrates well the positive impact that a company's activity can have. It also shows the collective interest represented by the company's innovation capacity. Abbe became a partner of Zeiss, and the operation of discoveries based on research subsequently became a distinctive trait of the company (on glass manufacturing, etc.). We can say that the company then had *de facto a* purpose of collective interest through the progress of optics. But it was not formalized. Upon Zeiss's death in 1888, his heirs had very different intentions, and Abbe came into conflict with them. He managed to buy out Zeiss's heirs' shares. But since then, he has ceaselessly sought to protect the purpose of the company concerning potential future buyers.

His solution was to transfer to a foundation, whose purpose he carefully drafted in a dedicated constitution, also providing a supervisory board with precise management rules and control of these rules. In 1896, the Carl Zeiss "Stiftung" (meaning "foundation" in German) was endowed with its articles of association. The Carl Zeiss Foundation, now the sole shareholder, must operate according to the very precise principles that Ernst Abbe took care to detail in a constitution that is 122 paragraphs long. This constitution assigns the company a mission of collective interest, but particularly innovation:

- to "cultivate the branches of precise technical industry, which have been introduced into Jena by the Optical Works and the Glass Works," and thereby promote the economic security of the employees and serve "the scientific and practical interest";
- "to promote the general interests of the branches of precise technical industry . . . and to take part in organizations and measures designed for the public good of the working population of Jena and its immediate neighborhood; to promote study in natural and mathematical sciences both as regards research and teaching."

This case seems exemplary of a company that formalizes in the constitution of its unique foundation-shareholder a purpose to protect from potential future shareholders the aims of the company and the promises it makes to its various constituencies (territory, employees, and society at large). The purpose here clearly designates the future that the company must seek to bring about and therefore the competencies it must build, beyond the simple production of optics. It is through its collective creation activity that it realizes its purpose.

But the case also shows all the precautions, rules, and oversight mechanisms that such a demanding purpose requires. In the constitution, the purpose has implications at all levels of management. For instance, investments should not be made based on their profitability alone, but only if they contribute to the learning and long-term viability of the company, taking into account all dimensions, including the interest of employees in their work. And the foundation's board, with representatives from the State of Saxe-Weimar and the university, is responsible for overseeing the company's management and ensuring that the purpose is respected.

The principle of shareholder foundations has spread a bit and is revitalized with the concept of "steward ownership" (Sanders, 2022). Today, we know of famous ones: NovoNordisk, Bosch, and so on. These companies are particularly interesting in the current context of alternative ways of organizing. But several warnings must be formulated.

First, the shareholder foundation presupposes that, at some point, a willing shareholder agrees to divest their shares to give them to a foundation. It is a demanding act and also prevents the possibility of raising capital by issuing new shares (except for sophisticated arrangements). We find this problem in the case of companies whose shares have been transferred to a trust in England. The case of John Lewis Partnership is known (Paranque & Willmott, 2014) but also shows the difficulties of such an arrangement when there is a need to recapitalize the company.

Second, most of the shareholder foundations we talk about today are very different from what Ernst Abbe created at Carl Zeiss in the beginning. A shareholder foundation can be a classic shareholder but one whose vocation is to use the dividends it draws from the company to serve a particular cause. This is the case, for example, of Patagonia. Yvon Chouinard, the famous founder of Patagonia, has transformed the legal structure of the company. In an open letter published in September 2022, Chouinard explains that he does not want to resort to any of the classic options available in the case of transmission: selling the company would not guarantee the future of the company and the interest of the employees. Taking the company public would push for short-term profit at the expense of the company's vitality and responsibility. So the option chosen is more radical: "earth is now our only shareholder," writes Chouinard (2022). In practice, the governance scheme separates ownership from control: On the one hand, 98 percent of the capital is transferred to Holdfast Collective in the form of nonvoting shares. This structure will hold 100 percent of the rights to the dividends and will use all profits for actions in favor of the environment. On the other hand, the remaining 2 percent of the capital corresponds to 100 percent of the voting rights. These voting rights and thus the control are entrusted to a "purpose trust," a governance structure that must guarantee respect for the company's mission, namely, "we're in business to save our home planet."

This case calls for two remarks:

- The foundation here is a shareholder, but it collects the dividends of the company to work for a cause outside the company. This scheme is therefore radically different from that of Carl Zeiss, where the purpose of the shareholder foundation was directly defining the purpose of the company's activities and what these activities should bring in the future to its different parties. The notion of a shareholder foundation must therefore be taken with caution.
- But Patagonia has also mobilized another structure, that of the purpose trust. It is a trust structure with as its beneficiary a purpose, rather than an individual or a group of beneficiaries. Here, we are closer to the structure of Zeiss. However, it should be noted that the mission is quite broad and potentially difficult to oversee. Most importantly, there is very little information about how the trust will operate, apart from the fact that the family will continue to appoint and control the board. In practice, it is unclear how the family will "guide" the purpose trust.

From this brief overview, we can draw several elements for discussion and research perspectives. On one hand, while the landscape was previously divided between nonprofit and for-profit organizations, there is already a range of intermediate paths where social and environmental purposes do not exclude profit. On the other hand, whereas in the twentieth century corporate reform projects primarily sought to politically rebalance governance by promoting the representation of different parties, various attempts – such as those of shareholder foundations – also aimed to enshrine and protect a purpose in the legal constitution of the company. However, today, new corporate forms are needed as we observe the rise of multiple responsibility-related challenges. There are now ecological issues to consider, as well as all the questions of general interest raised by the innovative activities of companies. Issues raised by digital platforms (surveillance society, privacy ...) or artificial intelligence, to name but a few, indicate that responsibility issues are multiplying. In this regard, alongside the path of integrating stakeholders in governance bodies or in ownership, incorporating purpose provides a way to impose the consideration of these issues in the management of future activities. We need to analyze how companies can practically articulate these multiple objectives and whether a constitutional purpose effectively promotes new and fruitful forms of deliberation. Research could play a central role here in enabling an informed and rigorous discussion of governance structures and the credibility of purposes.

4.2 Benefit Corporation and *Société à mission*: Two Contrasted Models

We would like here to contribute to this discussion on the governance structures that are appropriate for credible and enforceable purpose. We will do this by characterizing the profound variety of paths that are emerging within the international movement of purpose-driven corporations.

We still have little hindsight on this movement that began in Maryland in 2010 and now involves more than thirty-five states. It is challenging to provide a synthetic presentation of a field that is still evolving, especially since each state has adopted particular provisions. Obviously, the local economic and legal context is not neutral. Between the typical context of California, where fiduciary duties can be interpreted very narrowly, and the European context, where the interest of the company is interpreted much more broadly, the stakes are not the same. Similarly, there is a difference between a country where corporate social and environmental obligations are already very regulated and a much more liberal country.

We propose to present in more detail two contrasting cases: that of the benefit corporation and that of the *société à mission*. These two frameworks indeed convey two different logics or models that should be clearly distinguished, but which could be complementary.

4.2.1 Benefit Corporation: Disclosure Based on International Standards and Best Practices

The legal framework of benefit corporations is by far the most developed today, as it has been adopted in most US states as well as in British Columbia (Canada) and a few other countries. Italy, for example, has adopted a very similar framework with the *Società Benefit*. It is important not to confuse the benefit corporation with the "Certified B Corp" label: indeed, a benefit corporation is a legal corporate framework, whereas a B Corp is a company that has received certification, issued after an audit from a private organization.

The first benefit corporation was introduced in Maryland in 2010, with several other states following suit, including California (Clark & Babson, 2012; Murray, 2018; Vaughan & Arsneault, 2018). The benefit corporation was proposed by B Lab; B lab is a nonprofit organization founded in the United States in 2007 that also manages and issues the Certified B Corp label. To be certified, a company must demonstrate that it has a positive impact on "society" in the broad sense and on the environment. To award the B Corp label, B Lab requires a minimum score on an assessment grid that it has developed with the help of external experts, covering the main areas of CSR (governance, employees, community, environment). However, by asking directors to consider the impact of their decisions on various stakeholders, the label potentially exposes directors to lawsuits.

This was what initially motivated the proposal of constituency statutes in California, which we mentioned in Section 2. Following the governor's veto, B Lab proposed a new form of corporation, namely the benefit corporation. The idea was that, if shareholders adhere to a constitution that authorizes the pursuit of a broad purpose, directors would be protected from any legal action. To quote the argument developed by William Clark, the lawyer who drafted the model legislation for B Lab, "the creation of a new corporate entity provides additional legal clarity that the fiduciary duty of directors of a benefit corporation includes consideration of stakeholder interests and that shareholders have the right to enforce that standard of consideration" (Clark & Vranka, 2013).

To characterize this legal form, we will first discuss the content of its purpose before analyzing the governance structure adopted to enforce it. In what follows, we refer primarily to the law of benefit corporation in Maryland and to the model for benefit corporation legislation drafted by Clark, B Lab's lawyer (Clark & Vranka, 2013).

4.2.1.1 Regarding the Content of the Purpose

Benefit corporations must establish a purpose in their statutes that is a "general public benefit." In addition, they may also be allowed to pursue one or more "specific public benefit" purposes. General public benefit is defined as a "material, positive impact on society and the environment, taken as a whole, assessed against a third-party standard, from the business and operations of a benefit corporation."

It is interesting to understand how the evaluation frameworks are constructed. The challenge is to be able to evaluate the quality of a company's social and environmental practices and, if necessary, make visible the most virtuous companies. But by what criteria is a company considered virtuous, and what is considered "good practice"? Here we rely on the work of J. Lévêque, who has analyzed the B Lab assessment method in depth (Lévêque, 2022). In practice, though benefit corporations are not legally bound to a particular standard, B Lab offers an assessment grid that can be adapted by sector of activity, depending on the size of the company, and so on. This grid is organized around five themes ("impact areas"): Governance, Customers, Community, Environment, and Workers. And in each of these areas it establishes a list of good practices, each giving rise to points, by making an operational translation of major international standards, such as the international reference standard ISO 26000, the seventeen United Nations Sustainable Development Goals, the ten principles of the Global Compact, and the Global Reporting Initiative (GRI) Sustainability Reporting standards. These frameworks can be complemented by other standards or good practices at the sectoral or professional level. Beyond the operational impacts, the social or environmental interest or utility of the services or products made by the company is also considered, while other activities are considered as incompatible, typically tax evasion or certain activities such as the manufacture of weapons. There is obviously a whole range of activities or practices that are difficult to classify or that are considered "controversial." For instance, B Lab has set up an ad hoc procedure and delegates to a council of experts, namely the Advisory Committee, to conduct ad hoc investigations into these issues.

4.2.1.2 Regarding the Governance Structures

Benefit corporations include both a lock-in mechanism and accountability measures. Electing in or out of benefit corporation status is a voluntary act requiring a supermajority (two-thirds) vote of shareholders. In terms of accountability, the law establishes three important mechanisms. First, directors' fiduciary duties are expanded and require consideration of nonfinancial interests. Second, a benefit corporation has an obligation to report on its overall social and environmental performance as assessed against a comprehensive, credible, independent, and transparent third-party standard. Third, it is required to deliver an annual benefit report to the shareholders and to post it on its website so it is available to the public. As Clark and Vranka (2013) write, the objective of the "comprehensive" criteria is to ensure that "the corporation's impact on each of the non-financial interests that directors are required to consider is assessed in the annual benefit report."

It should be noted, however, that the law requires a self-report by the company, with no external audit. Furthermore, the benefit corporation does not imply any change in the governance structure itself.

Ultimately, the model of the benefit corporation can be described as a model of disclosure on standards of management. It is about integrating at the company level a discussion on the way in which the activities conducted are managed as well as on the social and environmental impact of these activities. Directors can no longer analyze activities under a strictly financial prism; they must also consider the responsible nature of these activities and their management. Here, the responsible character is evaluated against international standards and established good practices. Companies are thus invited to evaluate their relative positioning with respect to these norms. Typically, the company is led to question the minimum wages it offers, wage gaps within the company, social coverage, and so on. But the company is obliged only to specify the third-party evaluation framework it adopts and to publish its self-assessment against this framework. It should be noted that if a benefit corporation also has a specific mission, then reporting is discretionary.

Several authors have already warned that the benefit corporation offers weak protection for social and environmental objectives over time: not only do ownership structures remain unchanged but the accountability mechanisms promote transparency without forcing managers to adopt different approaches to resolve conflicts between objectives (Bandini et al., 2023; Blount & Offei-Danso, 2013; Ebrahim et al., 2014; Yosifon, 2017). Regarding enforcement, provisions have been added to the law in several states to prevent stakeholders from having any right to sue the company if the purpose is not met, that is, if the reporting shows poor consideration of the general public benefit. But we need to keep in mind that the intent of the drafters of the model was first to protect directors and managers willing to engage in social and environmental initiatives from potential shareholders' lawsuits.

4.2.2 Société à mission: Commitment to a Desirable Future

The emergence of the French *société à mission* occurred within a markedly different context. In Europe, generally, the risk of legal action against directors for not maximizing shareholder interests does not exist. The concept of fiduciary duties does not carry the same weight and it is well established that the interests of the company extend beyond those of the shareholders (referred to rather ambiguously as the *intérêt social* in France). It is generally observed that branches of labor and environmental law are more developed in European countries, with better-established social minimums. In the France case, the impetus for change then came more from the crisis of 2008 and more broadly from the realization that companies had significant potential for action in the collective interest, but that this potential could be hindered by limiting, or even deleterious, shareholder governance principles. This led to reflection in several circles, particularly at the

Collège des Bernardins, to question the foundations of the governance framework (Favereau, 2014; Segrestin & Hatchuel, 2012; Segrestin & Vernac, 2018; Segrestin et al., 2015). One result, taken up by the Notat and Senard report to the government in 2018, was to revisit the distinction between the concept of the enterprise – as an organization dedicated to collective creation – and the concept of the corporation, which is merely its legal clothes (Notat & Senard, 2018; Segrestin et al., 2021). If the enterprise is a distinctive type of economic but also creative organization, invented late, then it becomes possible to reconsider its legal attire. Here, the legal innovation of benefit corporations and FPCs has been an important source of inspiration. However, the French proposition took a different turn.

The objective was to define – through the purpose – the criteria under which management decisions could be considered legitimate at the level of each individual company. Indeed, each company had to be able to promote an original, innovative project and to pursue a particular desirable future. However, it was necessary to ensure that this project was clearly articulated, that it was genuinely oriented toward a collective interest, with a clear consideration of the related sustainability issues. And to integrate them into the constitutive rules of the company, that is, its constitution. The objective was to define the conditions under which management decisions can be considered legitimate at the level of each company. The challenge was both to secure and to stabilize the purpose by committing companies beyond any shareholder changes, while allowing businesses to define responsibility criteria in a way that is consistent with their activities.

Concretely, the 2019 law (the Loi PACTE [Plan d'Action pour la Croissance et la Transformation des Entreprises]) introduced three levels of change (see Box 4):

(1) It amended the definition of a company in the Civil Code by requiring that directors manage the company in its own interest, while considering the social and environmental issues related to its activities (Civil Code Art. 1833).
(2) It also introduced the possibility for any company to adopt a *raison d'être*. A *raison d'être* is defined as "the principles that the company adopts and for the observance of which it intends to allocate resources in the pursuit of its activities" (Art. 1835).
(3) Finally, it introduced a new status of company: any company, by virtue of Article L210-10 of the company law, can adopt the status of a *société à mission* (see the article in Box 4).

Box 4 The "société à mission," Art. L210-10 of the French company law (our translation)

A company can publicly declare itself a "société à mission" when the following conditions are met:

(1) Its articles of association (constitution) specify a *raison d'être* in accordance with Article 1835 of the Civil Code.
(2) Its articles of association (constitution) outline one or more social and environmental objectives that the company commits to pursue within the scope of its activities.
(3) Its articles of association (constitution) detail the procedures for overseeing the execution of the mission mentioned in point 2. These procedures stipulate that a mission committee, distinct from the corporate bodies provided for in this code and comprising at least one employee, is exclusively responsible for this oversight. The committee annually presents a report, appended to the management report per Article L232-1 of this code, to the assembly responsible for approving the company's accounts. The committee conducts any verifications it deems appropriate and has access to any document necessary for overseeing the mission's execution.
(4) The execution of the social and environmental objectives mentioned in point 2 is subject to verification by an independent third-party auditor, following procedures and disclosures defined by decree from the Council of State. This verification results in an opinion appended to the report mentioned in point 3.
(5) The company declares its status as a "société à mission" to the clerk of the commercial court, who publishes it, subject to the conformity of its statutes with the conditions mentioned in points 1 to 3, in the trade and companies register. The specific conditions for this publication are detailed by decree from the Council of State.

In September 2024, there were more than 1,700 registered *sociétés à mission*,[7] of all sectors and sizes. It can be noted that both large listed companies such as Danone and small companies in the social and solidarity economy sector are involved. Thus, cooperatives (Up, Socaps) and mutual organizations (Maif, Harmonie Mutuelle) have become mission-driven, thereby combining their

[7] See *Baromètre des sociétés à mission* – www.observatoiredessocietesamission.com/barometres-infographies/.

governance structures with the status of a *société à mission*. Let us now characterize this legal form by discussing first the content of its purpose and then the governance structure adopted to enforce it.

4.2.2.1 Regarding the Content of the Purpose

The purpose is defined both by the *raison d'être* and by the specific social and environmental objectives that detail it. The formulation is left entirely to the discretion of the company, making the purpose unique to each enterprise. Unlike benefit corporations, which refer to evaluation standards, the notion of *raison d'être* here is more about a unique identity and corporate project. Table 1 provides some examples of formulation, showing that the purpose signifies both what the company commits to preserving (a relationship with the territory, heritage, etc.) and what it commits to transforming or exploring (a more united society, healthier products, etc.).

Thus, on one hand, the law does not require a company to satisfy all its stakeholders, but it does ask it to declare the stakeholders to whom it commits. In this way, the classic difficulty of stakeholder approaches is circumvented. On the other hand, the law does not aim to define what is desirable in itself but rather acknowledges that companies may contribute to renewing what is considered desirable. In this way, it respects and even strengthens the freedom of enterprise: while companies created in the traditional corporate form risk having their purposes reduced, sooner or later, to the pursuit of profit and shareholder value, depending on changes in shareholders, the law here seeks to protect multiple and potentially very broad purposes. It thus allows a company to commit not only to already achievable objectives but to more ambitious objectives – which will require sustained efforts of exploration and for which there is no guarantee of results. This is one of the interests of the device: exploration capabilities are critical in the face of contemporary challenges. And if the company can contribute to the collective interest, it is not only by limiting its negative impacts but also through its ability to conduct in-depth research rigorously and to provide disruptive solutions to address transitions. Yet, it is indeed exploration and research expenditures that are the first to be cut when there is a need to extract more profit, as their return on investment is inherently uncertain and distant. Protecting the company's exploration capabilities is therefore essential.

The law is therefore highly flexible and open regarding the nature of the purpose, as the company wishing to become a *société à mission* freely defines its *raison d'être* and objectives. This flexibility makes this status a relatively generic legal framework: one could imagine, for example, a company committing to adhere to good conduct standards as outlined by frameworks such as

Table 1 Examples of the purposes of French sociétés à mission

	Key figures	***Raison d'être*** Social and environmental objectives written in the constitution
Danone	Listed company with 96,000 employees Sales of €27.7 billion	**"Bringing health through food to as many people as possible"** (1) Impact people's health locally with a portfolio of healthier products, with brands encouraging better nutritional choices, and by promoting better dietary habits. (2) Preserve and renew the planet's resources by supporting regenerative agriculture, protecting the water cycle, and strengthening the circular economy of packaging across its entire ecosystem in order to contribute to the fight against climate change. (3) Entrust Danone's people to create new futures: building on a unique social innovation heritage, give each employee the opportunity to impact the decisions of the Company, both locally and globally. (4) Foster inclusive growth by ensuring equal opportunities within the Company, supporting the most vulnerable partners in its ecosystem, and developing everyday products accessible to as many people as possible.
Maif	Insurance company with 8,000 employees and 4.2 million insured Sales of €4.5 million	**Convinced that only sincere attention to others and the world can guarantee a real common good, we, MAIF, place this attention at the heart of each of our commitments and each of our actions.** (1) Place the interests of its members at the heart of its activities. (2) Promote, through sincere attention, the fulfillment of its internal actors within a committed collective. (3) Contribute to the construction of a more solidarity-based society through its activities. (4) Contribute to ecological transition through its activities. (5) Promote the development of business models committed to seeking positive impacts.

Table 1 (cont.)

	Key figures	***Raison d'être*** Social and environmental objectives written in the constitution
Mirova	Institutional investor with 140 employees in 2020, 278 in 2024, and €31 billion under management	**Finance must serve as a tool to transform the economy into a model that preserves and restores ecosystems and the climate while fostering social inclusion, health, and well-being. To lead the way, we innovate throughout the entirety of our activities: investment, research, shareholder engagement, and influencing the financial community. We seek to combine environmental, social, and financial performance by placing our expertise in sustainable development at the core of all our investment strategies. To do so, we offer our clients solutions designed to develop their savings while contributing to a more sustainable and inclusive economy.** (1) Making positive impact a systematic objective of our investment strategies (2) Cultivating and developing our social and environmental expertise (3) Continuously innovating our products and approaches, always striving for impact (4) Supporting our stakeholders in their transformation toward a sustainable economy and finance (5) Applying the environmental and social standards we defend

B Corps. In that case, a *société à mission* would resemble a benefit corporation, but with a different governance structure.

Conversely, flexibility can be a limit. Several conditions for the effectiveness of the *société à mission* deserve to be highlighted. Typically, the purpose must be drafted precisely enough, yet without determining the strategy, to be engaging and controllable. One might wonder if norms for formulating the purpose should not prevail: for example, should there be systematic vigilance principles on sensitive issues depending on the company's activity? The French approach has been to promote the greatest corporate freedom so far, but this presumably requires, on the part of civil society, a challenge to learn to decipher missions well: what they commit to, but also, conversely, the subjects on which they remain silent . . .

4.2.2.2 Regarding the Governance Structures

Sociétés à mission include both a lock-in mechanism and accountability measures. Electing in or out of a *société à mission* is a voluntary act: The articles of association must be adopted, and if necessary amended, at the AGM with a supermajority of two-thirds.

The oversight mechanisms are quite original and differ from traditional models, such as disclosure or external audits. The *société à mission* imposes a dual level of oversight and a profound change in the company's governance itself. First, a mission committee must be established, distinct from existing governance bodies (e.g. the board of directors). This committee is charged with controlling that the strategy and management choices respect the commitments made in the purpose. The committee must include at least one employee and is endowed with significant investigative powers, as the law states that it "carries out any verification it deems appropriate and obtains any document necessary for overseeing the execution of the mission." The mission committee establishes an annual report that is attached to the report of the assembly approving the company's accounts. Second, an audit by an accredited external third party (an "independent third body") is also required for each *société à mission* at least every two years.[8]

Regarding enforcement, the *société à mission* therefore introduces a series of additional features compared to the benefit corporation. The law provides that if the independent third party's audit, also considering the mission committee's own assessment, declares that one of the social and environmental objectives of

[8] A company that employs fewer than fifty permanent employees during the fiscal year may provide in its bylaws that a mission officer replaces the mission committee. The mission officer may be an employee of the company, provided that their employment contract corresponds to an actual job position (L. 210-12).

the company is not met, then any party can sue the *société à mission* to require that it removes any mention that it is "*à mission*" (purpose-driven) from any media. It can therefore lose the right to be a *société à mission.* Additionally, if the chief executive makes decisions that are clearly incompatible with the constitutional purpose, then it can be judged as a management fault and two options may occur: either shareholders sue the CEO for breach of articles of incorporation, or stakeholders sue the company itself for this reason. This is why the legal character of the purpose is key, although the first mechanism, based on the third-party audit, allows that legal action is considered only as a last resort.[9]

The mission committee is undoubtedly the most original feature of the *société à mission*, together with the dual-level oversight. It is atypical, primarily because it constitutes a new internal board, with its members chosen by the company; however, it is also a board tasked with independently drafting a public report on the management's alignment with the purpose. This is not a committee representing stakeholders, but rather a board in charge of overseeing the quality of management decisions.

This mechanism is necessitated by the very nature of the purpose. The objective of the law was to encourage companies to commit to responsible and desirable futures. As a result, oversight becomes particularly challenging: it is no longer about measuring the impact of activities against generic criteria or verifying conformity with best practices. When the purpose involves desirable goals, for which solutions do not preexist and require intense exploratory efforts, the mission committee must assess the relevance and quality of these explorations. In comparison with benefit corporations, management may be evaluated not on good practices but rather on the quality of its explorations to find new ways of addressing social and environmental issues. Therefore, a new board is needed that can question management, but also engage with all parts of the company to analyze in depth any projects or processes. The mission committee can question the company on how it handles potential contradictions between profit objectives and social or environmental objectives, and how it explores possible ways to overcome them. At the same time, it must be capable of providing a rigorous and independent report. Empirically, it is interesting to note that the composition of these committees reflects these

[9] It is worth noting that the purpose does not enable the company to revise an existing contract: in French law, an executive (or the company) cannot withdraw from an agreement or a contract if the latter is deemed incompatible with the articles of incorporation (as the ultra vires doctrine might have allowed in early Anglo-Saxon corporate law). The constitutional purpose is therefore key for executives to refuse agreements if these may contradict the purpose *before* signing. And this has already happened for some companies.

challenges: in addition to employees, the committees often include academic researchers or external experts who are competent in the social and environmental issues identified by the purpose.[10]

However, it is also worth noting that the law provides no specific guidelines regarding the composition of the committee. Today, it appears that these committees very broadly and systematically call upon experts – for example academics or NGO members – who specialize in the issues covered by the missions. But could we accept a committee composed solely of internal members? Or shareholders? Potential deviations are imaginable, and therefore, there is also a challenge to develop, if not a new law, at least a doctrine and a practical code of the *société à mission*. This is what an association – the Communauté des Entreprises à Mission (CEM, roughly translated as "community of mission-driven companies") since 2019[11] – has dedicated itself to: this association brings together companies interested in the status, or already *sociétés à mission*, to share experiences, but also to professionalize methods (formulation of mission, method of oversight, etc.).

Table 2 compares the legal frameworks of benefit corporations (United States) and *sociétés à mission* (France). It highlights how these two frameworks embody different governance models.

In conclusion, we need to keep in mind that the movement of purpose-driven corporations is still in its early stages. But it is already taking on very diverse forms, whose ins and outs are important to understand thoroughly. It is therefore important to carefully study the contingency criteria that will favor the adoption of one legal framework over another in a particular state, and also how companies in practice are appropriating it, and potentially combining different accountability frameworks at their level. Danone, for example, has chosen to certify the entire group as a B Corp while also adopting the form of a *société à mission*. This example is not isolated, and the interest is evident because the B Corp framework allows alignment of its practices regardless of the requirements of local laws under which it operates its activities according to a common evaluation grid. Meanwhile, the *société à mission* will enable it to commit to its own unique trajectory of progress in social, health, and environmental matters.

[10] An ongoing study also shows that – out of a sample of 123 *sociétés à mission*, among the 22 that have a board of directors in addition to a mission committee – more than half (52 percent) have at least one academic on their mission committee (sometimes more); and that sustainability expertise is more represented in mission committees than in boards of directors (Acker, 2024). See also *Baromètre des sociétés à mission* – www.observatoiredessocietesamission.com/barometres-infographies/.

[11] To date there are approximately 1,800 *sociétés à mission* in France, with more than a million employees. This number is increasing rapidly. See www.observatoiredessocietesamission.com/barometres-infographies/

Table 2 Comparison of the main features of *sociétés à mission* and benefit corporations

Model	Disclosure based on shared standards	Commitment on a desirable future
	Benefit corporation (US[12])	*Société à mission* (France)
Directors' and management's duties	*Fiduciary duties* (duty of care, duty of loyalty)	*Fiduciary duties* + "The company is managed in its social interest, taking into consideration the social and environmental stakes of its activity (Civil Code Art. 1833)"
	Directors are expected to manage the company in the interest of the company *with consideration of stakeholders*	Directors are expected to manage the company in pursuit of the purpose
Purpose in the articles of associations (*constitutional purpose*)	***"General public benefit"*** Accountability on overall social and environmental performances + possibly a "specific public benefit"	***"Raison d'être"*** ("the principles the company gives to itself and for the respect of which it intends to allocate resources in the running of its activity") **+ *social and environmental objectives***
Lock-in mechanisms	Electing in or out requires a supermajority of two-thirds of votes	Electing in or out, or changing the purpose, requires a supermajority of two-thirds of votes
Governance structures		A mission committee, distinct from the board of directors, is in charge of overseeing the fidelity of management to the purpose
Accountability	Self-report including an assessment of the overall performance against a third-party standard	Annual report from the mission committee + Audit by an independent third party every two years

12 As presented in the white paper of Clark and Vranka (2013).

Nevertheless, and this deserves to be emphasized, the main risk of profit-with-purpose corporations as a whole consists in not providing an accountability mechanism consistent with the constitutional purpose. Benefit corporations are consistent when they demand self-evaluation against a third-party standard in relation to the "general public interest" they pursue. Similarly, the more demanding double level of oversight is consistent with the uniqueness of the purpose of *sociétés à mission*. But where the system is questionable is when there is no longer coherence. Typically, a benefit corporation can choose to adopt a "specific public benefit," but then it does not provide an appropriate oversight mechanism. Similarly, a company in France can define a *raison d'être* without becoming a *société à mission* and therefore without the associated oversight mechanisms. With the *société à mission*, which includes a board to monitor adherence to the mission and an independent audit, the risk of drift is reduced.

4.3 Section Conclusion: Key Elements

We saw earlier (Section 2) that the classic legal framework of the corporation is asymmetrical: while entrepreneurs may have social and environmental ambitions, the governance structure does not protect these ambitions over time. Future shareholders will always be able to challenge them. In light of contemporary challenges, it is essential for companies to be able to formulate and commit to a purpose that is not reducible to profit, without necessarily abandoning profit distribution. Profit and social/environmental objectives may seem antagonistic to one another. However, if a company commits to pursuing a social or environmental objective in addition to distributing profit, this implies that it refuses to choose between them or make compromises: it rather engages in a long-term effort of research and innovation to achieve both. It is probably because such efforts are necessary that the enterprise is of public interest today.

Nevertheless, the mere formulation of a purpose is not sufficient. For a purpose to be credible and for the company's commitment to be effective, appropriate governance structures are needed. Different governance structures are required depending on the nature of the purpose. And each one conveys a different representation of what is expected from corporate leaders and managers. We have highlighted various models. The cooperative pursues the interest of its members. Its governance is consistent with this objective: employees retain control because they hold the majority of the shares and the "one person = one vote" rule ensures the democratic expression of the members. The model of benefit corporations is very different: the governance structure remains largely unchanged compared to the classic corporation. However, a benefit corporation, whose purpose is to pursue a "general public benefit," commits to publishing an annual assessment of its social and environmental impacts based on an independent third-party standard. This is therefore a model aimed at transparency and reflective efforts by companies regarding their impacts. The case of the *société à mission* companies is different again: a *société à mission* defines in its articles of association the finalities of its activity, that is, its *raison d'être* with specific social and environmental objectives. To monitor the alignment of management decisions with these goals, a mission committee capable of conducting internal investigations is in charge of issuing an annual report on the adherence to the purpose. An external audit is also required every two years. This is therefore a framework to protect and enforce in a stable way, the pursuit of a certain desirable future.

Options regarding governance structures are multiplying today. Going forward, research will need to help us discern, beyond the purposes that companies claim, what their governance structures actually allow or do not allow to be protected and enforced over time. And while companies' inventiveness in terms of governance is already significant, public policies can play an important role in clarifying alternatives and restoring trust.

5 Conclusion: The Corporation and the Collective Interest

5.1 Private Enterprise, Public Activities

For decades, if not centuries, we have lived with the idea that the company manages its private affairs, and that it is legitimate that it pursues its own private interest, defining this interest as it sees fit, while the state, on its side, manages matters of public order and public interest. However, today it is clear that this division of roles is no longer sustainable (Scherer & Palazzo, 2007). Companies intervene in sectors or on missions traditionally assigned to the state (education, health, malnutrition, freedom of expression, space exploration . . .); they invest in and develop new types of infrastructure (e.g., the Starlink satellite constellation or the communicational infrastructures of social networks). For some, companies here significantly overstep their role, and this is what they denounce by talking about "corporate expansionism" (Caulfield & Lynn, 2024). Moreover, many of their projects could ultimately have a radical effect on relations between individuals, on the functioning of democratic life, or on the habitability of the planet . . . without anyone really knowing in advance whether these projects will be positive or deeply nightmarish. While in 1825 the first railway company in the United Kingdom – the Stockton and Darlington Railway – had as its motto *Periculum privatum utilitas publica* ("Private risk for public benefit"), today, the formula might be reversed for a great many companies: "Public risks for private benefits!"

This entanglement of public and private spheres is neither surprising nor problematic in itself and has, in fact, always existed, if only because business corporations, through their inventions and discoveries, contribute to renewing what is considered to be in the public interest. Nowadays, however, we are becoming increasingly aware that, within the classic legal framework, corporate activities are managed in the interest of the company – an interest whose definition can be left entirely to the discretion of shareholders, regardless of the impact of those activities on society and democratic life. Even if any billionaire, regardless of their disposition, could buy the shares of a company and decide its orientations.

Today, it is essential to reflect on the conditions in which the company can once again become a lever of collective interest. The problem is not to constrain the company or to prevent it from innovating. On the contrary. The problem is to restore what makes the enterprise of collective interest: namely, its ability to develop new resources or capacities – whether cognitive, technological, or financial – that can help address major contemporary challenges. Because it is not the market that creates wealth. Nor even really the production of goods or services. It is more the ability to invent new goods and new services to meet the needs of the population or ecological challenges.

5.2 The Purpose: Constitutionalizing Corporate Power

So far, two main approaches have been considered for this: CSR and public regulation. The principles of CSR, developed for several decades now, have had very positive effects within companies, but prove insufficient. Indeed, CSR developed precisely on the consideration that, fundamentally and in the long term, it was in the company's interest to take into account the expectations of its stakeholders. It assumed that shareholders, if they projected into the long term, would realize the importance of fair and balanced treatment of stakeholders. But this did not account for the shift of shareholders to institutional investors, whose long-term view is built not on one or a few companies but on hundreds of stock portfolios. More fundamentally, CSR was built on the idea of corporate responsibility "beyond legal obligations," that is, "beyond the law," and thus without changing the law or even questioning the possibility of changing the law. However, as we showed in Section 1, we must now recognize that the legal conditions for CSR are not met in classic corporate law: social and environmental initiatives – even the best-intentioned – are not protected.

If CSR is not enough, can we rely on the state to hold the company accountable? Undoubtedly, the state can define frameworks, as it historically did with labor law, and as it does today, for example, at the European level in terms of consumer protection, the environment, and so on. A series of international institutional initiatives is inspiring, facilitating, and guiding the progress of companies toward new conceptualizations of directors' duties and responsibilities. And these policy initiatives are reinforced by various efforts by financial markets and the civil society (Clarke, 2016). This is indispensable. But it remains insufficient. First, because there are many states and they are globally potentially quite powerless compared to companies. Second, because changing the duties of managers and what is legally expected from management is probably a condition for many sustainability policy initiatives to be effective. Then, and above all, because companies are constantly innovating, and it is actually impossible to regulate emerging areas by directing *ex ante* the paths of innovation dynamics. It is probably neither possible nor desirable for states to a priori define for all companies which scientific and technological developments are desirable or not!

The new path proposed by purpose-driven corporate forms is to change what is expected from management with appropriate structure of governance and accountability mechanisms to oversee management decisions. The corporation is not only a union of shareholders who defend their own interests. It is also and above all an organized collective of action, with a growing creative power. This creative power of organization and management has not been conceptualized in corporate law until now. Yet management must be all the more accountable as it is creative and transformative. The managerial authority of a company derives its legitimacy neither from ownership nor from traditional corporate law. The legitimacy of management could be more firmly grounded in law if a purpose was incorporated—i.e., defined in the corporate constitution. This constitutional purpose would outline the sustainable and collective-interest horizon that management must pursue, and for which it must therefore be accountable.

The principle of the purpose is thus to explicitly state within the very constitutive rules of the company, its constitution, the conditions in which the management of future activities can be legitimate. The constitutional purpose is a voluntary, unilateral commitment of the company, but which subsequently constrains the way its activities will be managed. It necessarily requires adequate accountability and governance structures. It is a "constitutional device," as defined by Caulfield and Lynn (2024). A constitutional device is defined for entities with power as "formally institutionalized means of constraining power and authority." Just as states impose limits on their power toward their subjects through constitutional rules (Robé et al., 2016), companies that adopt a purpose define rules that will frame their strategies and shape the management of their future activities.

We are undoubtedly only at the beginning. Much work remains to be done to define – through purposes – the principles of responsible management in the face of contemporary ecological challenges and the governance mechanisms needed to ensure adherence to them. The evolution of corporate law alone may not be sufficient. Effective transformation requires a change in corporate culture and governance for corporations to adopt a constitutional purpose. Nonetheless, we hope that this Element has contributed to showing that legal reforms can significantly contribute to it. The new corporate law can open new horizons for future entrepreneurs; it can also alter the perception of the role of managers and management education. And, more generally, it can contribute to redefining the role of the corporation in society.

References

Acker, V. (2024). *Identiques, différents ou les deux? Regard sur les organes de gouvernance des sociétés à mission à travers le prisme des compétences de leurs membres*. Master's thesis, ENS Paris-Saclay & Université Paris Saclay.

Aglietta, M., & Rebérioux, A. (2005). *Corporate Governance Adrift: A Critique of Shareholder Value*. Edward Elgar.

Aguilera, R. V., & Jackson, G. (2003). The cross-national diversity of corporate governance: Dimensions and determinants. *Academy of Management Review*, *28*(3), 447–465. https://doi.org/10.5465/amr.2003.10196772.

Arora, A., Belenzon, S., & Patacconi, A. (2018). The decline of science in corporate R&D. *Strategic Management Journal*, *39*(1), 3–32. https://doi.org/10.1002/smj.2693.

Asher, C. C., Mahoney, J. M., & Mahoney, J. T. (2005). Towards a property rights foundation for a stakeholder theory of the firm. *Journal of Management and Governance*, *9*(1), 5–32. https://doi.org/10.1007/s10997-005-1570-2.

Bandini, F., Boni, L., Fia, M., & Toschi, L. (2023). Mission, governance, and accountability of benefit corporations: Toward a commitment device for achieving commercial and social goals. *European Management Review*, *20*(3), 477–492. https://doi.org/10.1111/emre.12547.

Barnard, C. I. ([1938] 1968). *The Functions of the Executives*. Harvard University Press.

Battilana, J., & Dorado, S. (2010). Building sustainable hybrid organizations: The case of commercial microfinance organizations. *Academy of Management Journal*, *53*(6), 1419–1440. https://doi.org/10.5465/amj.2010.57318391.

Battilana, J., Lee, M., Walker, J., & Dorsey, C. (2012). In search of the hybrid ideal. *Stanford Social Innovation Review*, *10*(3), 51–55. https://doi.org/10.48558/WF5M-8Q69.

Battilana, J., Obloj, T., Pache, A.-C., & Sengul, M. (2022). Beyond shareholder value maximization: Accounting for financial/social trade-offs in dual-purpose companies. *Academy of Management Review*, *47*(2), 237–258. https://doi.org/10.5465/amr.2019.0386.

Belinga, R., & Guez, H. (2018). L'entreprise à l'épreuve de l'industrialisation de son actionnariat. In B. Segrestin & K. Levillain (eds.), *La mission de l'entreprise responsable: Principes et normes de gestion* (73–99). Presses des Mines.

Berle, A., & Means, G. ([1932] 1991). *The Modern Corporation and Private Property*. Transaction Publishers.

Berle Jr, A. A. (1931). Corporate powers as powers in trust. *Harvard Law Review, 44*(7), 1049–1074. https://doi.org/10.2307/1331341.

Besharov, M., & Mitzinneck, B. (2023). The multiple facets of corporate purpose: An analytical typology. *Strategy Science, 8*(2), 233–244. https://doi.org/10.1287/stsc.2023.0186.

Blair, M. M., & Stout, L. A. (1999). A team production theory of corporate law? *Journal of Corporation Law, 24*(4), 751–807. https://doi.org/10.2307/1073662.

Blair, M. M., & Stout, L. A. (2001). Trust, trustworthiness, and the behavioral foundations of corporate law. *University of Pennsylvania Law Review, 149*(6), 1735–1810. https://doi.org/10.2307/3312898.

Blount, J., & Offei-Danso, K. (2013). The benefit corporation: A questionable solution to a non-existent problem. *St. Mary's Law Journal 44*(3), article 2. https://doi.org/commons.stmarytx.edu/thestmaryslawjournal/vol44/iss3/2.

Boatright, J. R. (1994). Fiduciary duties and the shareholder-management relation: Or, what's so special about shareholders? *Business Ethics Quarterly, 4*(4), 393–407. https://doi.org/10.2307/3857339.

Cadbury, A. (1992). *Report of the Committee on the Financial Aspects of Corporate Governance*. GEE & Co.

Caulfield, M., & Lynn, A. (2024). Federated corporate social responsibility: Constraining the responsible corporation. *Academy of Management Review, 49*(1), 32–55. https://doi.org/10.5465/amr.2020.0273.

Chouinard, Y. (2022). A letter from Yvon Chouinard. Patagonia, September 14. www.patagonia.ca/stories/a-letter-from-yvon-chouinard/story-127258.html.

Ciepley, D. (2018). Can corporations be held to the public interest, or even to the law? *Journal of Business Ethics, 154*, 1003–1018. https://doi.org/10.1007/s10551-018-3894-2.

Ciepley, D. A. (2013). Beyond public and private: Toward a political theory of the corporation. *American Political Science Review, 107*(1), 139–158. https://doi.org/10.1017/s0003055412000536.

Clark, R. (1985). Agency costs versus fiduciary duties. In J. Pratt & R. Zeckhauser (eds.), *Principals and Agents: The Structure of Business* (55–79). Harvard Business School Press.

Clark, W. H., & Babson, E. K. (2012). How benefit corporations are redefining the purpose of business corporations. *William Mitchell Law Review, 38*(2), 817–851. https://open.mitchellhamline.edu/wmlr/vol38/iss2/8.

Clark, W. H., & Vranka, L. (2013). *White Paper: The Need and Rationale for the Benefit Corporation: Why It Is the Legal Form That Best Addresses the*

Needs of Social Entrepreneurs, Investors, and, Ultimately, the Public. https://shorturl.at/CHDL2.

Clarke, T. (2016). The widening scope of directors' duties: The increasing impact of corporate social and environmental responsibility. *Seattle University Law Review, 39*(2), 531–578.

Clarke, T. (2020). The contest on corporate purpose: Why Lynn Stout was right and Milton Friedman was wrong. *Accounting, Economics, and Law: A Convivium, 10*(3), 20200145. https://doi.org/10.1515/ael-2020-0145.

Clarke, T. (2021). *Corporate Governance: A Survey*. Cambridge University Press.

Commons, J. R. (1919). *Industrial Goodwill*. McGraw-Hill.

Davis, J. H., Schoorman, F. D., & Donaldson, L. (1997). Toward a stewardship theory of management. *Academy of Management Review, 22*(1), 20–47. https://doi.org/10.5465/amr.1997.9707180258.

Deakin, S. (2012). The corporation as commons: Rethinking property rights, governance, and sustainability in the business enterprise. *Queen's Law Journal, 37*(March), 339–381.

Djelic, M.-L. (2013). When limited liability was (still) an issue: Mobilization and politics of signification in 19th-century England. *Organization Studies, 34*(5–6), 595–621. https://doi.org/10.1177/0170840613479223.

Dodd, E. M. J. (1932). For whom are corporate managers trustees? *Harvard Law Review, XLV*(7), 1145–1162. https://doi.org/10.2307/1331697.

Donaldson, L., & Davis, J. H. (1991). Stewardship theory or agency theory: CEO governance and shareholder returns. *Australian Journal of Management, 16*(1), 49–64. https://doi.org/10.1177/031289629101600103.

Donaldson, T. (2002). The stakeholder revolution and the Clarkson principles. *Business Ethics Quarterly, 12*(2), 107–111. https://doi.org/10.5840/beq200212211.

Donaldson, T., & Preston, L. E. (1995). The stakeholder theory of the corporation: Concepts, evidence and implications. *Academy of Management Review, 20*(1), 65–91. https://doi.org/10.5465/amr.1995.9503271992.

Ebrahim, A., Battilana, J., & Mair, J. (2014). The governance of social enterprises: Mission drift and accountability challenges in hybrid organizations. *Research in Organizational Behavior, 34*, 81–100. https://doi.org/10.1016/j.riob.2014.09.001.

Fama, E. F., & Jensen, M. C. (1983a). Agency problems and residual claims. *Journal of Law and Economics, XXVI*(2), 327–349. https://doi.org/10.1086/467038.

Fama, E. F., & Jensen, M. C. (1983b). Separation of ownership and control. *Journal of Law and Economics, XXVI*(2), 301–325. https://doi.org/10.1086/467037.

Favereau, O. (2014). *Entreprises: La grande déformation*. Parole et Silence, Collège des Bernardins.

Fayol, H. (1917). *Administration Industrielle et Générale*. Dunod et Pinat.

Ferran, E. (1999). *Company Law and Corporate Finance*. Oxford University Press.

Freeman, E. R. (1988). A stakeholder theory of the modern corporation. *Perspectives in Business Ethics Sie*, 3(144), 38–48.

Friedman, M. (1970). A Friedman doctrine – The social responsibility of business is to increase its profits. *New York Times*, September 13. www.nytimes.com/1970/09/13/archives/a-friedman-doctrine-the-social-responsibility-of-business-is-to.html.

Galbraith, J. K. ([1967] 1989). *Le nouvel état industriel*, 3rd ed. Gallimard.

Gartenberg, C. (2022). Purpose-driven companies and sustainability. In G. George, M. R. Haas, H. Joshi, A. M. McGahan, & P. Tracey (eds.), *Handbook on the Business of Sustainability: The Organization, Implementation, and Practice of Sustainable Growth* (24–42). Edward Elgar.

Gelter, M. (2009). The dark side of shareholder influence: Managerial autonomy and stakeholder orientation in comparative corporate governance. *Harvard International Law Journal*, *50*(1), 129–194. https://ssrn.com/abstract=1352414.

Gide, C. (1924). *Le programme coopératiste et le salariat: Trois leçons du cours sur la coopération au Collège de France*. Association pour l'enseignement de la coopération.

Goyder, G. (1951). *The Future of Private Enterprise: A Study in Responsibility*. Basil Blackwell.

Goyder, G. (1987). *The Just Enterprise*. Andre Deutsch.

Grandori, A. (2001a). "Cognitive failures" and combinative governance. *Journal of Management and Governance*, *5*(3–4), 252–260. https://doi.org/10.1023/a:1014040221634.

Grandori, A. (2001b). Neither hierarchy nor identity: Knowledge-governance mechanisms and the theory of the firm. *Journal of Management and Governance*, *5*(3–4), 381–399. https://doi.org/10.1023/a:1014055213456.

Grandori, A. (2022). Constitutionalizing the corporation. In R. E. Meyer, S. Leixnering, & J. Veldman (eds.), *The Corporation: Rethinking the Iconic Form of Business Organization* (57–76). Emerald.

Grandori, A., & Furlotti, M. (2019). Contracting for the unknown and the logic of innovation. *European Management Review*, *16*(2), 413–426. https://doi.org/doi:10.1111/emre.12291.

Guinnane, T. W., Harris, R., Lamoreaux, N. R., & Rosenthal, J. L. (2008). Business organisation in the long run: An international history of private limited companies [*Pouvoir et propriété dans l'entreprise: Pour une histoire internationale des sociétés à responsabilité limitée*]. *Annales: Histoire, Sciences Sociales*, *63*(1), 73–108. https://doi.org/10.1017/s039526490002388x.

Gulati, R. (2022). *Deep Purpose: The Heart and Soul of High-Performance Companies*. Harper Business.

Hatchuel, A. (1994). Frédéric Taylor: Une lecture épistémologique. L'expert, le théoricien, le doctrinaire. In J.-P. Bouilloud & B.-P. Lecuyer (eds.), *L'invention de la gestion, Histoire et pratiques*. L'Harmattan.

Hatchuel, A., & Segrestin, B. (2007). La société contre l'entreprise? Vers une nouvelle norme d'Entreprise à progrès collectif. *Droit et Société*, *65*, 27–51. https://doi.org/DOI:10.3917/drs.065.0027.

Hatchuel, A., & Segrestin, B. (2019). A century old and still visionary: Fayol's innovative theory of management. *European Management Review, 16*(2), 399–412. https://doi.org/10.1111/emre.12292.

Hatchuel, A., & Segrestin, B. (2020). Devoir de vigilance: La norme de gestion comme source de droit? *Droit et société, 106*(3), 667–682. https://doi.org/10.3917/drs1.106.0667.

Hauriou, M. (1899). *Leçons sur le Mouvement social données à Toulouse en 1898*. Librairie de la société du receuil général des lois et des arrêts.

Henderson, R. (2020). *Reimagining Capitalism in a World of Fire*. Portfolio Penguin.

Henderson, R. (2021). Innovation in the 21st century: Architectural change, purpose, and the challenges of our time. *Management Science*, *67*(9), 5479–5488. https://doi.org/orcid.org/0000-0001-5902-1891.

Hernandez, M. (2012). Toward an understanding of the psychology of stewardship. *Academy of Management Review, 37*(2), 172–193. https://doi.org/10.5465/amr.2010.0363.

Hiller, J. S. (2013). The benefit corporation and corporate social responsibility. *Journal of Business Ethics*, *118*(2), 287–301. https://doi.org/10.1007/s10551-012-1580-3.

Jacoby, S. M. (2004). *Employing Bureaucracy: Managers, Unions, and the Transformation of Work in the 20th Century*, revised ed. Taylor & Francis.

Jensen, M. C., & Meckling, W. H. (1976). Theory of the firm: Managerial behavior, agency costs and ownerships structure. *Journal of Financial Economics*, *3*(4), 305–360. https://doi.org/10.2139/ssrn.94043.

Johnston, A., Segrestin, B., & Hatchuel, A. (2019). From balanced enterprise to hostile takeover: How the law forgot about management. *Legal Studies*, *39*(1), 75–97. https://doi.org/10.1017/lst.2018.32.

Kaufman, A. (2002). Managers' double fiduciary duty: To stakeholders and to freedom. *Business Ethics Quarterly, 12*(2), 189–214. https://doi.org/10.2307/3857810.

Khurana, R. (2007). *From Higher Aims to Hired Hands: The Social Transformation of American Business Schools and the Unfulfilled Promise of Management as a Profession*. Princeton University Press.

Klettner, A. (2021). Stewardship codes and the role of institutional investors in corporate governance: An international comparison and typology. *British Journal of Management, 32*(4), 988–1006. https://doi.org/10.1111/1467-8551.12466.

Knight, F. (1921). *Risk, Uncertainty, and Profit*. Hart, Schaffner, & Marx; Houghton Mifflin.

Lan, L. L., & Heracleous, L. (2010). Rethinking agency theory: The view from law. *Academy of Management Review, 35*(2), 294–314. https://doi.org/10.5465/amr.2010.48463335.

Lazonick, W. (2014). Profits without prosperity. *Harvard Business Review, 92* (9), 46–55. https://hbr.org/2014/09/profits-without-prosperity.

Lazonick, W. (2023). *Investing in Innovation: Confronting Predatory Value Extraction in the U.S. Corporation*. Cambridge University Press.

Lefebvre-Teillard, A. (1985). *La Société anonyme au 19ème*. Presses Universitaires de France.

Leixnering, S., Doralt, P., & Meyer, R. E. (2022). The past as prologue: Purpose dynamic in the history of the Aktiengesellschaft. In R. E. Meyer, S. Leixnering, & J. Veldman (eds.), *The Corporation: Rethinking the Iconic Form of Business Organization*, Research in the Sociology of Organizations vol. 78 (97–120). Emerald. https://doi.org/10.1007/s10551-020-04439-y.

Le Masson, P., & Weil, B. (2008). La domestication de l'innovation par les entreprises industrielles: L'invention des bureaux d'études. In A. Hatchuel & B. Weil (eds.), *Les nouveaux régimes de la conception* (53–69). Vuibert.

Lévêque, J. (2022). *Concevoir la mission comme un engagement génératif: Enjeux, écueils et principes de formulation pour les sociétés à mission*. Presses des Mines.

Levillain, K. (2012). La flexible purpose corporation: Un petit pas pour le juriste, un grand pas pour l'entreprise? *Cadres-CFDT, 450–451*(Septembre), 15–24.

Levillain, K. (2017). *Les entreprises à mission: Un modèle de gouvernance pour l'innovation dans l'intérêt commun*. Vuibert.

Levillain, K., Segrestin, B., & Hatchuel, A. (2019). Profit-with-purpose corporations: An innovation in corporate law to meet contemporary CSR challenges. In A. McWilliams, D. E. Rupp, D. S. Siegel, G. K. Stahl, & D. A. Waldman (eds.),

The Oxford Handbook of Corporate Social Responsibility: Psychological and Organizational Perspectives (490–513). Oxford University Press.

Levillain, K., Segrestin, B., Hatchuel, A., & Vernac, S. (eds.). (2020). *Entreprises, Responsabilités et Civilisations: Vers un nouveau cycle du développement durable*. Presses des Mines.

Lohmeyer, N., & Jackson, G. (2024). Vocabularies of motive for corporate social responsibility: The emergence of the business case in Germany, 1970–2014. *Business Ethics Quarterly, 34*(2), 231–270. https://doi.org/10.1017/beq.2022.45.

Lopes, H. (2022). The deontic basis of the firm: Implications for corporate governance. *European Management Review, 19*(4), 598–607. https://doi.org/10.1111/emre.12506.

Luyckx, J., Schneider, A., & Kourula, A. (2022). Learning from alternatives: Analyzing alternative ways of organizing as starting points for improving the corporation. In R. E. Meyer, S. Leixnering, & J. Veldman (eds.), *The Corporation: Rethinking the Iconic Form of Business Organization*, Research in the Sociology of Organizations vol. 78 (209–231). Emerald.

Mac Cormac, S. H. (2011). New corporate forms: Flexible purpose corporations, benefit corporations, and L3Cs. www.law.berkeley.edu/files/bclbe/Berkeley_Handout_1182011_-_1.pdf.

Mac Cormac, S. H., & Haney, H. (2012). New corporate forms: One viable solution to advancing environmental sustainability. *Journal of Applied Corporate Finance,24*(12), 1–8. https://doi.org/10.1111/j.1745-6622.2012.00378.x.

Mahoney, J. T. (2023). Corporate personhood and fiduciary duties as critical constructs in developing stakeholder management theory and corporate purpose. *Strategy Science, 8*(2), 212–220. https://doi.org/10.1287/stsc.2023.0191.

Mair, J., & Rathert, N. (2021). Alternative organizing with social purpose: Revisiting institutional analysis of market-based activity. *Socio-Economic Review, 19*(2), 817–836. https://doi.org/10.1093/ser/mwz031.

Mair, J., & Wolf, M. (2021). Hybrid organizations as sites for reimagining organizational governance. In G. Donnelly-Cox, M. Meyer, & F. Wijkström (eds.), *Research Handbook on Nonprofit Governance*(311–325). Edward Elgar.

Mair, J., Wolf, M., & Ioan, A. (2020). Governance in social enterprises. In H. K. Anheier & T. Baums (eds.), *Advances in Corporate Governance: Comparative Perspectives* (180–202). Oxford University Press.

Marens, R. (2008). Recovering the past: Reviving the legacy of the early scholars of corporate social responsibility. *Journal of Management History, 14*(1), 55–72. https://doi.org/10.1108/17511340810845480.

Margolis, J. D., & Walsh, J. P. (2003). Misery loves companies: Rethinking social initiatives by business. *Administrative Science Quarterly, 48*(2), 268–305. https://doi.org/10.2307/3556659.

Mayer, C. (2013). *Firm Commitment: Why the Corporation Is Failing Us and How to Restore Trust in It?* Oxford University Press.

Mayer, C. (2018). *Prosperity: Better Business Makes the Greater Good*. Oxford University Press.

Mayer, C. (2019). The purpose and future of the corporation. Speech given at the Mossavar-Rahmani Center for Business and Government, Harvard Kennedy School, February 21. www.hks.harvard.edu/sites/default/files/centers/mrcbg/files/Mayer_2.19.19.transcript.pdf.

McMahon, C. (2013). *Public Capitalism: The Political Authority of Corporate Executives*. University of Pennsylvania Press.

Meyer, R. E., Leixnering, S., and Veldman, J. (eds.). (2022). *The Corporation: Rethinking the Iconic Form of Business Organization*, Research in the Sociology of Organizations vol. 78. Emerald.

Mitchell, R. K., Agle, B. R., & Wood, D. J. (1997). Toward a theory of stakeholder identification and salience: Defining the principle of who and what really counts. *Academy of Management Review, 22*(4), 853–886. https://doi.org/10.5465/amr.1997.9711022105.

Murray, S. M. (2018). Explaining the adoption of benefit corporation laws by the US states. *Journal of Financial Economic Policy, 10*(3), 351–368. https://doi.org/10.1108/jfep-09-2017-0085.

Notat, N., & Senard, J.-D. (2018). *L'entreprise, objet d'intérêt collectif* (Mars). La Documentation française. www.ladocumentationfrancaise.fr/rapports-publics/184000133-l-entreprise-objet-d-interet-collectif.

Nyland, C., Bruce, K., & Burns, P. (2014). Taylorism, the International Labour Organization, and the genesis and diffusion of codetermination. *Organization Studies, 35*(8), 1149–1169. https://doi.org/10.1177/0170840614525388.

Orrick, UnLtd, & Thomson Reuters Foundation. (2014). *Balancing Purpose and Profit: Legal Mechanisms to Lock In Social Mission for "Profit with Purpose" Businesses Across the G8*. www.trust.org/wp-content/uploads/2024/09/downloaded_file-121.pdf.

Orts, E. W. (1992). Beyond shareholders: Interpreting corporate constituency statutes. *George Washington Law Review, 14*(1), 14–135.

Paranque, B., & Willmott, H. (2014). Cooperatives – saviours or gravediggers of capitalism? Critical performativity and the John Lewis Partnership. *Organization, 21*(5), 604–625. https://doi.org/10.1177/1350508414537622.

Peaucelle, J.-L. (2003). *Henri Fayol, Inventeur des outils de gestion: Textes originaux et recherches actuelles*. Economica.

Reich, L. S. (1985). *The Making of American Industrial Research: Science and Business at GE and Bell, 1876–1926*. Cambridge University Press.

Robé, J.-P. (1999). *L'Entreprise et le Droit*. Presses Universitaires de France.

Robé, J.-P. (2011). The legal structure of the firm. *Accounting, Economics, and Law: A Convivium, 1*(1), 1–86. https://doi.org/www.degruyter.com/view/j/ael.

Robé, J.-P., Lyon-Caen, A. & Vernac, S. (2016). *Multinationals and the Constitutionalization of the World Power System*. Routledge.

Saleilles, R. (1897). *Les accidents de travail et la responsabilité civile: (Essai d'une théorie objective de la responsabilité délictuelle)*. Arthur Rousseau.

Sandberg, J. (2011). Socially responsible investment and fiduciary duty: Putting the Freshfields Report into perspective. *Journal of Business Ethics, 101*(1), 143–162. https://doi.org/10.1007/s10551-010-0714-8.

Sanders, A. (2022). Binding capital to free purpose: Steward ownership in Germany. *European Company and Financial Law Review, 19*(4), 622–653. https://doi.org/10.1515/ecfr-2022-0020.

Scherer, A. G., & Palazzo, G. (2007). Toward a political conception of corporate responsibility: Business and society seen from a Habermasian perspective. *Academy of Management Review, 32*(4), 1096–1120. https://doi.org/10.5465/amr.2007.26585837.

Schneiberg, M. (2011). Toward an organizationally diverse American capitalism? Cooperative, mutual, and local, state-owned enterprise. *Seattle University Law Review, 34*(4), 1409–1434.

Schneiberg, M. (2013). Movements as political conditions for diffusion: Anti-corporate movements and the spread of cooperative forms in American capitalism. *Organization Studies, 34*(5–6), 653–682. https://doi.org/10.1177/0170840613479226.

Segrestin, B. (2017). When innovation implied corporate reform: A historical perspective through the writings of Walther Rathenau. *Gérer et Comprendre – English language online edition, 2*. www.annales.org/gc/GC-english-language-online-edition/2017/SEGRESTIN.pdf.

Segrestin, B., & Hatchuel, A. (2011). Beyond agency theory, a post-crisis view of corporate law. *British Journal of Management, 22*(3), 484–499. https://doi.org/10.1111/j.1467-8551.2011.00763.x.

Segrestin, B., & Hatchuel, A. (2012). *Refonder l'entreprise*. Le Seuil.

Segrestin, B., Hatchuel, A., & Levillain, K. (2021). When the law distinguishes between the enterprise and the corporation: The case of the new French law on corporate purpose. *Journal of Business Ethics, 171*, 1–13. https://doi.org/10.1007/s10551-020-04439-y.

Segrestin, B., Hatchuel, A., & Starkey, K. (2020). Captains of industry? Value allocation and the partnering effect of managerial discretion. *Management and Organizational History, 15*(4), 295–314. https://doi.org/10.1080/17449359.2021.1877558.

Segrestin, B., Johnston, A., & Hatchuel, A. (2019). The separation of directors and managers: A historical examination of the status of managers. *Journal of Management History, 25*(2), 141–164. https://doi.org/doi:10.1108/JMH-11-2018-0060.

Segrestin, B., & Levillain, K. (2023). Profit-with-purpose corporations: Why purpose needs law and why it matters for management. *European Management Review, 20*(4), 733–740. https://doi.org/10.1111/emre.12628.

Segrestin, B., Levillain, K., & Hatchuel, A. (2022). Management and law: The forgotten contribution of P. Selznick. *M@n@gement, 25*(1), 69–78. https://doi.org/10.37725/mgmt.v25.8521.

Segrestin, B., Levillain, K., Vernac, S., & Hatchuel, A. (eds.). (2015). *La Société à Objet Social Etendu: Un nouveau statut pour l'entreprise*. Presses des Mines.

Segrestin, B., & Vernac, S. (2018). *Gouvernement, participation et mission de l'entreprise*. Herman.

Selznick, P. (1969). *Law, Society, and Industrial Justice*. Russell Sage Foundation.

Sjåfjell, B., Johnston, A., Anker-Sørensen, L., & Millon, D. (2015). Shareholder primacy: The main barrier to sustainable companies. In B. Sjåfjell & B. J. Richardson (eds.), *Company Law and Sustainability: Legal Barriers and Opportunities*. Cambridge University Press.

Sharma, A. (1997). Professional as agent: Knowledge asymmetry in agency exchange. *Academy of Management Review, 22*(3), 758–798. https://doi.org/10.5465/amr.1997.9708210725.

Sternberg, E. (2000). How the strategic framework for UK company law reform undermines corporate governance. *Hume Papers on Public Policy, 8*(1), 54–68.

Szramkiewicz, R. (1989). *Histoire du droit des affaires*. Montchrestien.

Taylor, F. W. (1895). A piece-rate system, being a step toward partial solution of the labor problem. *Transactions of the American Society of Mechanical Engineers, 16*, 856–903. https://doi.org/10.1115/1.4061210.

Taylor, F. W. (1911). *Principles of Scientific Management*. Harper & Brothers.

Thomsen, S., Poulsen, T., Børsting, C., & Kuhn, J. (2018). Industrial foundations as long-term owners. *Corporate Governance: An International Review, 26*(3), 180–196. https://doi.org/10.1111/corg.12236.

Vaughan, S. K., & Arsneault, S. (2018). The public benefit of benefit corporations. *PS: Political Science and Politics, 51*(1), 54–60. https://doi.org/10.1017/S1049096517001391.

Veldman, J., & Willmott, H. (2019). What is the corporation and why does it matter? *M@n@gement, 16*(5), 605–620. https://doi.org/10.3917/mana.165.0605.

Veldman, J., & Willmott, H. (2022). Social ontology of the modern corporation: Its role in understanding organizations. In R. E. Meyer, S. Leixnering, & J. Veldman (eds.), *The Corporation: Rethinking the Iconic Form of Business Organization*, Research in the Sociology of Organizations vol. 78 (165–190). Emerald.

Ventura, L. (2023). New trends in legal frameworks for purpose-driven companies: The European way(s). *European Management Review, 20*(4), 725–732. https://doi.org/10.1111/emre.12627.

Yosifon, D. G. (2017). Opting out of shareholder primacy: Is the public benefit corporation trivial? *Delaware Journal of Corporate Law, 41*(2), 461–508. https://doi.org/10.2139/ssrn.2733880.

Cambridge Elements

Corporate Governance

Thomas Clarke
UTS Business School, University of Technology Sydney

Thomas Clarke is Professor of Corporate Governance at the UTS Business School of the University of Technology Sydney. His work focuses on the institutional diversity of corporate governance and his most recent book is *International Corporate Governance* (Second Edition 2017). He is interested in questions about the purposes of the corporation, and the convergence of the concerns of corporate governance and corporate sustainability.

About the Series

The series Elements in Corporate Governance focuses on the significant emerging field of corporate governance. Authoritative, lively and compelling analyses include expert surveys of the foundations of the discipline, original insights into controversial debates, frontier developments, and masterclasses on key issues. Its areas of interest include empirical studies of corporate governance in practice, regional institutional diversity, emerging fields, key problems and core theoretical perspectives.

Cambridge Elements

Corporate Governance

Elements in the Series

Asian Corporate Governance: Trends and Challenges
Toru Yoshikawa

Value-Creating Boards: Challenges for Future Practice and Research
Morten Huse

Trust, Accountability and Purpose: The Regulation of Corporate Governance
Justin O'Brien

Corporate Governance and Leadership: The Board as the Nexus of Leadership-in-overnance
Monique Cikaliuk, Ljiljana Eraković, Brad Jackson, Chris Noonan and Susan Watson

The Evolution of Corporate Governance
Bob Tricker

Corporate Governance: A Survey
Thomas Clarke

Board Dynamics
Philip Stiles

The Role of the Board in Corporate Purpose and Strategy
Robert Bood, Hans van Ees and Theo Postma

Investing in Innovation: Confronting Predatory Value Extraction in the U.S. Corporation
William Lazonick

Incorporating Purpose: The New Legal Foundations for the Corporation and Its Management
Blanche Segrestin, Kevin Levillain and Armand Hatchuel

A full series listing is available at: www.cambridge.org/ECG

For EU product safety concerns, contact us at Calle de José Abascal, 56–1°, 28003 Madrid, Spain or eugpsr@cambridge.org.

www.ingramcontent.com/pod-product-compliance
Ingram Content Group UK Ltd.
Pitfield, Milton Keynes, MK11 3LW, UK
UKHW022144080726
473066UK00010B/747
* 9 7 8 1 0 0 9 6 2 3 5 1 3 *